What Readers Are Saying

"In this profoundly intimate and soul-baring memoir, Deborah Marqui reveals how her tenacious journey through cancer transcended her physical healing. At its heart, *From The Fire Into The Garden: A Healing Journey* reaffirms, in compelling fashion, the power of faith, family, friends, self-compassion and surrender to the grace of God and the healing power of Nature in the face of suffering. It is also a testament to Deb's remarkable attunement to the transformative lessons to be learned from one's body, mind and spirit. For those facing similar ordeals, Deb's presence in the telling of her story will hold you through your journey. For those of us faced with the prospect of never living fully, her story sends a message of hope. By the time you finish soaking up her story, you will have a sense that Deb has invited you to sit with her as she takes in the beauty of her Healing Gardens."
~ Jim Otepka, LMFT, Psychotherapist, Former Director, Tri City Family Services

"Deborah takes us on a healing journey through one of humanity's greatest challenges. By her example, she teaches us all as she embraces her vulnerability with the innocence of a lamb, the courage of a lion, and the wisdom of an elder."
~ Pamela Verner LCSW

"Deb Marqui writes with fierce honesty about her journey through cancer in search of physical health, emotional solace, and spiritual connection. Like a long, beautifully written letter from a close friend, the book is intimate, personal, and *true*, in the deepest sense. It will speak to each reader directly. Ultimately, we are all in need of healing, and this book vividly describes how one woman struggled and persevered, finding her own unique path to healing through modern medicine, nature, grace, and love."
~Jack Lloyd, Contemplative Outreach Chicago - Circle of Service

"Deborah offers us an intimate look at her healing journey with profound wisdom and vulnerability. Through her pain and fear Deborah shows us how God uses stillness and nature to lead to healing. It is a journey that touches all our lives, showing how to walk with Love."
~ JoAnne McElroy, MA, Spiritual Director, Enneagram Presenter

"*FROM THE FIRE INTO THE GARDEN: A HEALING JOURNEY* by Deborah Marqui is an intimate and honest memoir of one woman's physical, emotional, psychological and spiritual search for healing from cancer. This book touches the reader on many levels, providing valuable wisdom for self-understanding, courage in the face of adversity, and personal empowerment. The creation of Healing Gardens, the author's "earth school," is particularly inspirational as a metaphor for life and a blessing to all who enter it. I can immediately think of seven people I would enthusiastically give this book to."
~ Lindsey Huddleston, M.A., M.A., Licensed Professional Counselor

"Deb Marqui takes the reader into the world of being fully present to a confrontation with mortality. Going beyond the physical challenge of cancer, this is a story for anyone with emotional or spiritual challenges. In other words, this is for anyone living in the human condition. Full of honesty and vulnerability, the wisdom discovered during Marqui's journey with cancer is a course on living."
~ Phil Jackson, Chaplin, Former Contemplative Outreach Coordinator Chicago Chapter

"In *From The Fire Into The Garden: A Healing Journey*, Deb Marqui shares her powerful story and specifies the steps we can use to bring healing to all dimensions of our lives, whether we are dealing with a cancer diagnosis, or the many other challenges that come with being human. I have been blessed to have known Deb

for fifteen years and to witness many aspects of her evolution. She truly walks the walk. In this book, Deb shares with great skill, honesty and insight, the secrets of healing that we can all access if we are willing."
~ Marianne Cirone, MS, MFA, CYT 500, Founder, Editor, *Integrative Cancer Review*

"A heart wrenching read of a spiritual journey which Deb had grown into from the traumatic physical trials of coping with deadly cancer. The only way through the journey is to keep opening to a greater reality than we find in our battle, a reality of a new being, a True Person brought forth by the touch, embrace, and love of our life. The constant practice of a contemplative opening of the heart through the activity of daily living is all we can do, and Deb's story yielded a supreme gift of God's grace and love."
~ Alan Krema, Contemplative Outreach Chicago Chapter Coordinator.

"Deborah Marqui welcomes you in with an open heart and disarming honesty. Through vivid storytelling and keen spiritual sensitivity, each chapter brings forth the unfolding of comfort, wisdom and hope. She remains relatable, while gently guiding the way through redemptive suffering using nature, centering prayer, and authentic community. Full of beautifully articulated truth, you'll want to reach for this book again and again."
~ Susan Borgstrom, MA, ACC, Director, Awakening in Nature

From the Fire Into the Garden:

A Healing Journey

From the Fire Into the Garden:

A Healing Journey

By

Deborah Marqui

Nature's Path Publishing Company

ISBN: 9780692099223

To my loving and supportive husband, Buzz.
To our children, Matthew, Nicholas, Alyce and Melinda.
And their spouses.
And to all my descendants.
Thank you for the joy you have brought me and
the life lessons you have taught me.

"Remember one thing, said Badger. The stories people tell have a way of taking care of them. If stories come to you, care for them. And learn to give them away where they are needed. Sometimes a person needs a story more than food to stay alive. That is why we put these stories in each other's memories. This is how people care for themselves."

~Barry Lopez, **Crow and Weasel**

Table of Contents

Reflection

*"The story reveals the meaning of what would
otherwise be an intolerable event."*
~Hannah Arendt

Ahh, the lazy days of August. August is usually the hottest, most sultry month of all in the Midwest, yet today is cool and sunny. It is such a welcome relief as the heat all summer long has been uncharacteristically brutal. I take a moment to give thanks. By habit, I have retreated, with a cup of tea in hand, to the small deck behind our home. The wonderful, fresh smell of Nature and the luscious gardens, now in full bloom, spread out before me. A tiny 'sweat bee' joins me and rests on the binding of my journal. It's as if she knows my name – Deborah, which in Hebrew means 'bee.' Perhaps she is here to remind me of my long, arduous journey from *doing* to *being.* On these mornings when the silence is so silent – a glorious state, the sweet nature of the gardens embraces me.

I look around again and see with new eyes what arose from the ashes of a devastating cancer diagnosis – Healing Gardens – two acres of perennial gardens and a beautiful, primitive wooded area. I remember with perfect clarity, a lovely day in June, with weather very much like today, twenty-four years ago, when the journey began.

It was a Friday afternoon in early June of 1995. And, as it was every Friday, all of the therapists, me included, who worked at the addiction outpatient facility met in a large room to review our cases of the week, especially the difficult ones that had a dual diagnosis. Not only were they addicted to alcohol or drugs, they also struggled with other mental health issues. As the meeting proceeded in the windowless staffing room, my mind wandered, thinking of the weekend ahead and the gorgeous weather outside. In the Midwest, our summer days are all too fleeting, and I longed to breathe in the fresh air and feel the warm sun on my skin.

I was new at this, and it had been a long week for me. I had seen eighteen individual clients, was facilitating three different therapy groups, and teaching an ongoing series about the disease of alcoholism. The cases were complex and demanding, and as a newly-minted therapist, my skills were being tested at every turn. That afternoon, as my coworkers continued with their case presentations, I put my elbow on the long conference table and rested my head in my left hand. My eyelids got heavy and I thought that if I were not careful, I just might fall asleep.

As I considered getting up to pour myself a cup of coffee, my fingers brushed over a small lump on the back of my neck. *How strange*, I remember thinking. I had never noticed it before. It didn't really hurt and I was able to move it a little between my fingers. I wasn't frightened or concerned, but I made a mental note to make an appointment to ask my doctor about what it might be. I had always been healthy. I was forty-eight years old, married, with four children – two sons, Matt and Nick, twenty-one and nineteen, and two daughters, Alyce and Mindy, sixteen and ten. Having just completed my graduate degree in social work at the University of Illinois at Chicago one year ago, and now a full-time therapist at this addiction recovery center, and working toward being a Licensed Clinical Social Worker, my life was more than full.

Dying was the furthest thought from my mind.

Chapter 1 – The Diagnosis

And I said to the angel who stood at the gate of the year: "Give me a light so I may safely tread in to the unknown." And he replied: "Go out into the darkness, and put your hand in the hand of God. That shall be to you better than a light and safer than a known way."
~Minnie L. Haskins, 1908

I made an appointment with my general practitioner early the next week. He examined the lump and recommended a ten-day round of antibiotics, thinking the lump might be an infection of some kind. Every morning when I rubbed in my face lotion, I would slide my hand down my neck to check the progress of the lump. When I completed the full prescription and nothing had changed, my doctor strongly recommended that I have the lump removed and biopsied. He referred me to a respected surgeon in the area.

My sister, Laurie, with her analytical mind and science background, graciously accompanied my husband, Buzz, and me to meet the surgeon, Dr. Lee, whose office was conveniently close to our home. She was a petite and lovely lady. Her soft-spoken manner radiated kindness. I didn't feel this a learned technique, but more from her Asian ways. At our first meeting, she gently felt the lump and agreed that it should be biopsied.

In a gentle, reassuring voice she said, "Try not to jump to any conclusions. The lump may be nothing at all, perhaps just a benign, harmless cyst."

Laurie, Buzz and I nodded, understanding the wisdom of her suggestion. I noticed her beautiful, graceful, small hands and thought that her surgery stitches would probably be tiny and neat with very little scaring. After we left, I asked Laurie if she had noticed, and she nodded. The following week under a local anesthetic, the doctor performed the biopsy at a surgery center close by her office. We were told the tissue sample, along with her report of the operation, would be sent to the lab. The results would be back in a few days. In her account of the operation, she wrote, 'The patient tolerated the procedure well.'

A few days later, I was in the kitchen making breakfast for my daughter when the phone rang. It was Dr. Lee's receptionist who asked to speak to me.

"Dr. Lee would like both you and your husband to come into the office tomorrow. Would 2:30 p.m. be all right?"

My heart sank. My mind started racing. *Oh my God, she wants to see both of us, the news cannot be good.*

I could feel my voice shake as I tried to get it out loud enough for her to hear. Fear had moved in on me. Finally, I agreed to the time, then asked, "Are the results back from the lab?"

She replied, "Yes, the labs have come back."

I knew she could not give me the results and at that moment, I didn't want to know. The next day, Buzz and I drove to her medical building. Without delay, we were ushered into her private office. Holding hands, we sat side by side. I looked at Buzz and the dread spread across his face. I wondered if he could see it on me. Soon, Dr. Lee came in clutching a medical folder. She pulled up a chair and sat right in front of us, almost knee to knee. In a tender and soft voice, she told us the devastating news.

"I'm very sorry to tell you that you have a cancer called non-Hodgkin's lymphoma."

Buzz and I looked at each other and our voices came out as one, "What is that?"

Briefly, Dr. Lee explained, "Non-Hodgkin's lymphoma is a cancer that starts in cells called lymphocytes, which are part of the body's immune system. Lymphocytes are in the lymph nodes that are all over your body and other lymphoid tissues, such as the spleen and bone marrow."

I could feel the tears come as we both peppered her with questions, but she held up her hand. "I know you have lots of questions, but I recommend that you see a cancer specialist. I do not want to give you inaccurate information." She went on to say, "I am new to the area, so I do not have a specific cancer oncologist to recommend. There are some wonderful oncologists in the city [Chicago], but it may take several weeks to get an appointment."

That evening, still reeling from the shocking news, and with tears streaming down my face, I wrote my first journal entry about this cancer:

June 22, 1995 The Diagnosis~

I am on a journey, like the ship on the cover of my journal. I am open and ready to learn. I found out today I have non-Hodgkin's lymphoma. "Forty-eight is so young to have this cancer," the surgeon said. "Most people who are diagnosed with this kind of cancer are in their seventies and eighties."

Upon hearing the words that I have cancer, the dreaded disease that I heard about as a child, I let the tears flow. I vividly remember, hushed voices, tears, snippets of conversation. "There was blood in the toilet. He won't last long." My parents watched my Dad's best friend, who was married with five children, die of colon cancer at the age of 35. I played with their oldest daughter, Mary Kay.

5

My head is whirling with these memories as I try to digest this shocking news. Buzz, sits quietly. As this news sinks in, his eyes well with tears.

Earlier that day, my younger sister, Abby, burst in the door crying as soon as she heard the news. In a loud angry voice, she exclaimed, "You will lick this fucking disease!" On her way to see me, she had prayed to God to give her comforting words for me. She was a little embarrassed about what came out of her mouth. Those words were the perfect words for Abby to say. She is a 'got your back' kind of person and will fight to make things right for anyone. After she left, I wondered: *Why couldn't those be God's words? God hates disease as much as we do.* All of my siblings and I had been taught to fear God as children. There was always the threat of hell if we died with a mortal sin on our soul, but somewhere along the way, God had become more accessible, or maybe I had grown to understand God's presence more.

God's 'overwhelming self' was all around me, and within me that night in bed. After writing about the momentous life-changing news of the day, I put down my journal and turned off the light. There was a soft summer breeze coming through the opened window with an earthy scent that enveloped the room. I snuggled next to Buzz and I could sense God in my husband's gentle snoring as he lay next to me; in my concerned, loving family, in my peaceful home, in my faithful friends. Feeling hugged by God, I cried with joy. I recognized with absolute clarity how blessed I was. In a very strange way, I was feeling an excitement about this journey, a journey I really wasn't ready for. I had no idea what to expect, and I knew it would be rocky. God had given me a gift to seek truth and wisdom and now I was stepping forward. Yes, I was ready.

Although in a state of shock, I was surprised by what I experienced that day and my reaction to this devastating news. In the past, I had experienced God's hand in my life and so, in the midst of my tears and terror, a knowing grew in my heart that God's Grace would continue to guide me. God did not zap me with cancer to make me learn life's lessons. Disease is a part of living on this Earth. Carolyn Myss, a true spirit in holistic and spiritual health, says God's guidance and direction is everywhere in this 'earth school.' We only need to have eyes that see and ears that hear. A life-threatening illness will, if we choose, wake us up to life.

As the waves of shock rolled through me, a feeling of sheer helplessness settled in. I remembered a friend of mine, Nancy, who had been diagnosed with breast cancer. She had found great solace in Bernie Siegel's book, *Love Medicine & Miracles*. I quickly purchased a copy and began to read. Through my studies and spiritual seeking, I knew there was a strong connection between the body, mind and spirit and I was determined to learn more. I had been born into a strict Catholic family where there were many rules to follow in order to spend eternity in heaven. My recent explorations into a more spiritual and deeper existence had opened up many new doors that spoke more about the love of God rather than the fear of God. I told myself I wasn't 'cheating' on my faith, just taking it to a new level. Now I was ready to explore. I hadn't thought it would come to me in such a way. I had pictured more of a gentle path of exploration. I felt like I had somehow been dumped at a trailhead and told this is the time. Get started.

Dr. Lee recommended Chicago for an oncologist. The city was an hour away and I could not imagine waiting two weeks to see someone. We were desperately anxious to learn more about this cancer (this was before we were computer literate.) We looked in the local phone book under oncology. One doctor was listed in our area. I quickly called and took the first available appointment, which was several days later.

While people were planning their long July 4th weekend, Buzz and I were sitting in the waiting room of the oncologist's office. Laurie soon joined us.

"Don't worry, Deb," Laurie said. "We will find out all we need to know to beat this thing." She had already begun to research treatment protocols for this disease and had brought a thick file folder.

We had only been there a short time when a young nurse came out of a doorway and called my name. She ushered us into the consultation room without Laurie. I wondered if Laurie should come, too. *What is the protocol? How many people are 'allowed' in the doctor's private office?* But the moment passed and although I knew Laurie wanted to come, I didn't invite her in. Later, I wished I had. What we experienced was heartless, rendering both of us speechless and numb.

The doctor's office was of moderate size with shelves filled with books on both sides of the room and windows facing the street. A large walnut desk was in the middle of the room facing the door. He was seated behind his desk. In his early fifties, with moderate build, thinning brown hair and large glasses, he rose to shake our hands and introduce himself while pointing to the two chairs in front of his desk. We sat down and waited for him to speak.

Clearing his throat, he glanced down at the results of the biopsy and began to speak, his voice flat and expressionless, like a college professor to his students, "Your biopsy shows that your lymphocytes have the features that are consistent with malignant lymphoma, follicular mixed large cell and small cleaved cell type. Essentially, you have cancer of the lymph nodes, which are all over your body." He paused and looked at us for a moment, then added, "Unfortunately, you have small-cleaved cells mixed in with the large cells. The small-cleaved cells are indolent and stubborn. No matter what treatment you pursue, the cancer will return."

We stared at him wordlessly, and as though we did not understand.

He added, "There is no cure for this cancer."

Moments passed as Buzz and I tried to take this in, a heavy silence enveloping the room.

Not believing I heard him correctly, I finally asked, "There is no treatment for this cancer? Not even chemotherapy?" I watched him as he slowly got up from his chair and sat in front of us on the edge of his desk.

"You can do a round of chemotherapy, but the cancer will eventually come back."

In shock and disbelief, we sat immobilized with the dreaded question lurking in the silence. Still sitting on the edge of his desk, his leg swinging back and forth, I wondered *Does he want us to leave? Is this conversation over?*

I had to know. Buzz and I clasped hands.

"What is the prognosis?"

Nonchalantly, as if he had just delivered a weather report, he replied, "Since there is no definable, successful treatment protocol, you can expect to live five to seven years."

Buzz and I stood and held each other and cried. He looked away.

We finally mumbled something about getting in contact with him later and left.

We tearfully delivered the news to Laurie in the waiting room. Laurie shook her head and said nothing while

9

rooting around in her file. She held up a medical pamphlet on cancer research and opened it to a graph that had wavy lines.

"Look, look!" she said, sounding very much like our mother when she was intent on making us see something important. "This picture graphs a bell curve of different cancers and their prognosis. Look at the bottom of the bell curve."

Buzz and I looked, trying to make sense of what she was trying to show us.

"This graph shows that ten percent of cancer patients experience spontaneous remissions and no one knows how or why."

After the dark experience in the doctor's office, we walked out of the office into the warm, summer day. Somehow, I saw light, maybe a ray of hope, or was it just anger at the coldness of this doctor? I knew right then I would do whatever I could to prove him wrong.

Laurie was the first to speak, "We will *not* be going back to that doctor."

This was our initiation into the world of Western medicine, where some doctors might know about treating disease, but know little about the human spirit. Looking back over time, I had often wondered why every minute detail of this man and his office was so indelibly imprinted on my memory. He was such a shallow, cold person, lacking in compassion, the most important ingredient of anyone in the medical profession, but even more importantly, I now realize these many years later, this was the day I decided I had a choice.

I could believe what he told me and die as he said or I could find another path. From that point on, as I reflected on my experience, he became known to me as Dr. Death. The more I read about treating cancers holistically, the angrier I became. How dare he tell me when I will die! Didn't he know I could handle the truth or hear the possibilities – but not without hope? If a trusted physician suggests your case is hopeless, what chance is there of healing? I needed the positive thoughts and energy from my chosen doctor, one who believes as I do, in the power of prayer, and the strength and resiliency of the human spirit. It took me a long time to forgive Dr. Death for playing God and putting me in a box without hope. However, this anger contained strong energy that served me well. I wanted to prove him wrong. With renewed resolve, Buzz, Laurie and I jumped into the vast, titanic world of cancer research, treatment, and healing.

Chapter 2 – The Journey Begins

"It's your road, and yours alone, others may walk it with you, but no one can walk it for you."

~Rumi

While Buzz started to research alternative, holistic treatments, Laurie researched treatment protocols at major teaching hospitals. What a great team! Buzz and Laurie made up the opposite sides of the 'healing coin.' Laurie with her Western, focused scientific mind and Buzz with the intuitive, alternative-healing proponent. I began to look inward. Up to this point in my life, studying to be a psychotherapist, and interested in having a spiritual connection, I had read extensively and knew there was a connection between the body, mind and spirit. Helping others to integrate these into wholeness was my motivation for becoming a psychotherapist and ultimately opening a private practice. However, I did not know how to accomplish this balance in my own life! I could talk the talk, so to speak, but I wasn't walking the walk.

I was shocked into the awareness of this gross imbalance by the cancer diagnosis and yet, there was a part of me that wasn't too surprised. I would often shift my thinking to *when I have more time I will eat better. When I have time, I will look at this urge to be perfect. When I have more time, I will introduce more spiritual food into my life.* Now I knew it was time to look deeply into each area of my life.

No one is certain about the etiology of cancer, although researchers agree that stress, heredity, nutrition, and environment (exposure to toxicity) all play a part. Those memories of being called inside on hot summer evenings in the middle of a kick ball game, or hide and seek began to surface. In response to our outraged cries, my parents would explain the truck would soon be going through spraying for mosquitoes. From the windows, we would wait for the truck and watch the toxic spray spread through the trees, like the angel of death in the movie, *The Ten Commandments*. (The movie portrayed the angel of death as a creeping mist. As the mist passed by each Egyptian household, the first-born male in each family would die. But the angel of death would Passover all the Jewish families with the blood of a lamb smeared above the front door.) The mosquito spray would come through the cracks in the old windows of our house and we would turn up our noses at the acrid smell. More memories surfaced of my wallpapering and painting business – painting with oil-based paints for thirteen years prior to starting graduate school and all the home rehab jobs Laurie and I worked on as young, married women.

Prior to the cancer diagnosis, I often skipped lunch while at work, and might have popcorn for dinner in the interest of squeezing in another client. Oblivious, my mind was full of negative thoughts about others and of myself. I was caught in a vicious, habitual loop. And, spiritually I was stagnant.

I had read a book called, *When the Well Runs Dry* years before. The author, Thomas Green, used the metaphor of a dried up well to explain what happens when we do not cultivate our spiritual life. When a well pump is not primed, the water becomes cloudy or stagnant and finally dries up. Just like what can happen to the spiritual life. We even can have beautiful, meaningful spiritual experiences and in the busyness of life, forget them. Spiritually, I had become like the old, dry, hand-dug well on our property.

Now came the time for healing, a complete healing. I wanted to be healed physically, mentally, and spiritually – not just cured of cancer. From my reading, I knew that messages and beliefs that we hold inside about ourselves affect our behavior and often do not serve life. I could often help others find these messages, but could I help myself? Were there any messages I fed my body that aided in the formation of this cancer? What were the lessons I needed to learn? These questions began the walk through the 'fire of cancer.'

"To transform we must be willing to touch our suffering, to look deeply with intuitive eyes to see and understand our nature."
~James Finley

Chapter 3 – The Tools of Healing

*"I love to think of Nature as an unlimited broadcasting station, through
which God speaks to us every hour,
if we will only tune in."*
~George W. Carver

That fateful day I was diagnosed, I was certain of two things. First, I needed to keep a cancer journal. Journaling was a familiar practice. In my early twenties I learned this valuable tool as a way to make sense of the endless chatter running rampant in my brain. Journaling took this 'monkey mind' out of my head, where I could make more sense of what was happening to me. And now, needing a place to put all the endless questions for the doctors, the internal questions for myself, and important information for anyone who was part of my healing, this practice was invaluable. Second, I knew for certain I needed a meditation practice, to help me slow down and become grounded.

I chose to journal and meditate looking out over Nature. Because of this seemingly small inconsequential decision, I slowly came to know Nature as alive, knowing and always speaking. Into the fall and winter months as the cancer treatment progressed, too weak and sick to be in Nature, I sat in silence observing the landscape and animal activity outside my window.

In the stillness and solitude, I began to 'hear' Nature speaking. I noticed the leaves seemed to fall so effortlessly, gently letting go into the next phase of re-birth, and I wondered, *have I surrendered to the fact of the cancer diagnosis, not giving up, but surrendering to what is?* Observing the playfulness and tenacity of squirrels became a delight to witness, reminding me of the importance of laughter. Watching the first snowfall, immersed in the quiet stillness, gave me a whole new understanding of the word *peaceful*. Simply observing the landscape outside my window, Nature became a major teacher providing me lessons about life, God, and myself. By the time chemotherapy was over, a new sensation grew in my heart, I could not wait to *be* in Nature and become a participant. I re-awakened to the strength and healing power of Nature that I first experienced as a child.

My love affair with Nature began when I was quite young, watching my mother bring whatever was currently blooming into our house. We had lilacs, bridal wreath and forsythia in the spring. She loved to put huge branches in large antique jardinières around the house. At times, she could not wait and would cut the branches in February to 'force' the growth, especially forsythia. After about ten days in water, the small bright yellow blossoms appeared. After the flowers died, pale green delicate leaves opened.

Picking whatever she could find in the small backyard and in the woods behind our house and, of course, along the side of the road, she created lovely arrangements, especially around the holidays. She collected beautiful vases of all shapes, colors and sizes so she could select the perfect container to match the foliage and flowers she had at hand. As the arrangements began to droop, she pulled out any parts that were still alive and put them in a smaller vase continuing this process until all the foliage had died. In this small act, Mom taught me about the life and death cycle, but especially her commitment and reverence for life.

When I was eight or nine, I vividly remember her asking me to go out along the side of the driveway and pick lilacs. Using a rake, I pulled the tall branches down to pick the delectable blooms. To me, the scent was a piece of heaven. Now, struggling with my health issues, I knew I needed to journey a great distance with Nature at my side to re-discover the senses I lost somewhere on my road to adulthood.

Chapter 4 – Healing Begins

June 1995

*"...everything can be taken from a man but one thing: the last of the
human freedoms – to choose one's attitude in any given set of
circumstances, to choose one's own way."*
~Viktor Frankl

Upon approaching fifty, I had been thinking about my
body, moaning and groaning about all the imperfections,
remembering how I 'used to' look. There had been a time
when I was happy with my body, but maybe it was all a veneer
– just the surface, as this disease hadn't just appeared
overnight.

As a first step toward healing I decided to journal
about what I liked about my body now (a Bernie Siegel
suggestion.) What did I like? I still liked the shape of my
somewhat sagging breasts, my behind, which Buzz described
as 'perky,' my soft stomach, as a result of four wonderful
pregnancies, my feet, even with a small bunion forming on
one toe, my small hands, beginning to wrinkle with age spots,
yet, still strong, my smile, my hair, which was still thick and
chestnut colored, my blue green-eyes that seemed to be getting
smaller, and my legs along with the small veins that have
come out of nowhere.

Writing what I liked about my body was a difficult
exercise, but I wanted to stop the critical and judgmental
thinking about myself, and this was a good start. I was angry
my body had let me down, but thinking of my body as an
adversary was pointless. This body housed my soul – and as a
friend's young son told her, "Where the mind goes, the body
will follow." Later, deep into treatment as I realized the extent

of my poor eating habits, lack of exercise, and taking my body for granted, I even asked my body's forgiveness. What I was really doing was forgiving myself, which began the long journey of loving me with all of my frailties and imperfections. No matter what happened to my body over the next eight months, my mantra became, *I am on a healing journey for which I am grateful.*

Reflecting about how I had abused my body over the years along with a continuous stream of denigrating remarks, I remembered a paper I had written in graduate school. The assignment was to construct a 'genogram,' of my family of origin, which consisted of going back as far as I could remember, listing traits, characteristics, descriptors of everyone in my family, both maternal and paternal side. From this exercise, family patterns of behavior, both positive and negative family traits became clear. I could see which family traits empowered or disempowered, and, from that vantage point, decide to make changes. My intention was not to blame my parents, they did the best they could with what they were given. My intention was to become conscious.

From my perspective as the third child in this large, Catholic family, with nine siblings, (six girls and three boys), our home was governed by three rules:

1. Control – one must be in control of feelings and behaviors – crying was frowned upon, and 'looking good' was most important no matter what you were feeling on the inside.
2. An unspoken 'No-talk' rule. We did not talk about what we needed, wanted, or felt. Feeding, clothing and shelter was considered most important. My parents did not see us as having emotional needs.
3. Work comes first – play holds little importance.

With German roots from both parents, there was a strong emphasis on structure, work, and keeping your feelings to yourself. There was also a concern that if you praised a child too much, they would develop 'a big head' and become too self-absorbed. Yet, from my mother's Irish roots, came the strong message that 'looking good' no matter what, was paramount. I could see how I had tried to look good, yet seldom received the message that I had succeeded in looking good!

One Easter morning in 1954 when I was eight years old, I was particularly excited about wearing my Easter outfit. The night before I had carefully set out my outfit, some of which was handed down, but I did not care. Everything was cleaned and pressed, and Mom had purchased a new white sailor hat for me, with a navy-blue ribbon around the crown. I also had an almost new pair of black, patent leather shoes with a grosgrain bow on the toe and a strap that went around my ankle. They were too small for my sister, but perfect for me. In preparation for Mass, I polished them with Vaseline so they would shine.

Carefully, I began putting on my thin cotton slip, then my white pleated skirt and the navy-blue jacket with six brass buttons down the front, three on each side. I slipped into my beautiful shoes, folding over the toes of my new white anklet socks that were a little too big. Hidden in my dresser drawer, out of reach of my younger siblings, I retrieved a small white plastic purse with a brass clasp that had been sent to me by my Aunt Sophie. Upon receiving this most grown-up accessory, I searched and searched through the house to find just the right items to fill my purse. What would a beautiful grown-up girl have in her purse? I wondered. The contents finally included one of my Dad's small black combs, toilet paper (for Kleenex), a nickel and a few pennies, a small broken mirror, a rosary and a tiny book about the Saints. I would endlessly rearrange the items and pretend I needed something important from my purse.

Putting the sailor hat on my head, I adjusted the elastic string underneath my chin, then put on my new white gloves and placed my purse over my arm and went into my Mother's bedroom for her approval and inspection. I was not disappointed as she exclaimed, "You look wonderful! You must go show your Father!"

Excited, I went downstairs and found Dad already dressed for church reading the newspaper in the kitchen. Shyly, in a small voice, I asked, "Dad, how do I look?"

For a few moments, he did not put down the paper. I thought he did not hear me, but then he looked up and said flatly with a little impatience, "Oh. You look nice," and went back to reading the paper.

I don't think I ever asked him again for his opinion on how I looked, even on my wedding day. For me, my Father was unable to fulfill one of the most important roles of a Dad – to assure his daughter that she was beautiful, capable and intelligent and had everything she needed to make it in the world with or without a man.

My parents married in their mid-twenties in Springfield, Illinois, on July 26, 1941. Mom was the oldest of seven children – and the only girl. Dad was the youngest of nine children. Compared to many, my childhood was idyllic. Born in 1946, I was the third oldest of ten children with eight biological and two foster siblings. I grew up with two older sisters, three younger brothers, and four younger sisters. A good Catholic family, my mother had seven children in nine years.

They adopted the standard parental roles of that era – Dad was the breadwinner who took charge of all the finances and Mom was a homemaker. Encouraged by my mother, his number one priority was his job. For years, I labeled Dad a workaholic, but have come to the realization that by today's standards, he would not be placed in that category. He was home by six o'clock almost every evening and on the weekends. However, with his emotional distancing and preoccupation with endless projects at home, in some respects he might as well have been absent. My mother supported him in his work and school. At the age of thirty-five, Dad received his Master's Degree in Education and eventually became a superintendent of a nearby school district. Mom never questioned her role until years later when feelings of anger and resentment surfaced over Dad's preoccupation with the children in the school district, to the exclusion of her needs and their own troubled and somewhat delinquent children.

My younger brother, John called my two older sisters, Ann (Andrea) and Laurie (Laurette), and me 'The Big Three.' My two older sisters and I were born about a year apart, and then two years later, my brother John and two years after that, my brother Ted. My sisters, Felicity, Corinne (Bunnie), and Abigail (Abby) were born over the next five years, along with the addition of two foster children, Bill and Frances. Because we were the oldest, we were allowed to have experiences that my younger siblings could not – there was good reason why my brother called us 'The Big Three.'

As children, the only vacation my father would take was to Springfield, Illinois to visit my parent's relatives over a four-day weekend. The younger children stayed with my parents in my grandparents' large, two-story home. My two older sisters and I stayed with Aunt Mimi, my grandfather's unmarried sister, in a quaint, tall, old, brick building called, Hickox Apartments. Mimi would often be at my grandparents' home awaiting our arrival. Shortly after greeting and hugging

25

my grandparents, Paw Paw, my grandfather, would drive my two sisters, Aunt Mimi and me to Mimi's apartment several miles away in downtown Springfield. The streets in Springfield were paved with bricks and Paw Paw's car would vibrate with this strange, bumpy sound.

As one entered the large lobby, there was a pleasant smell of old furniture and a slight musty smell of carpet. She lived on the third floor, so as a child this was my first introduction to riding an elevator. Side by side, there was a passenger and freight elevator, which was large to accommodate furniture, and had a heavy, folding iron door. Mimi often took the freight elevator if the passenger one was in use. I was frightened at first and held Mimi's hand as the massive box began to go up with strange, creaking noises. I watched each floor pass by until it stopped at the third floor. My sisters and I often argued over whose turn it was to press the elevator button.

Mimi's apartment was magical. To us, it was doll size, with a living room, a small dressing room with a drawer full of scarves that we could play with, a small bathroom and a kitchen the size of a tiny rectangular closet – she did all her work in the kitchen sitting on a stool. Her appliances were about the size of my kindergarten 'play kitchen.' She served us cookies and milk before bed and she even had an air conditioner! I remember asking, "Mimi, where is your bed?"

She laughed. "Here it is!" and walked over to the closet, opened the door and pulled down her bed. My two sisters and I slept in the Murphy bed and she slept on the couch. All these wonderful details I would relate to my younger brother in grand detail.

Along with special treatment from my parents, the three of us older girls had many caretaking responsibilities for our younger siblings, and we did not always use a gentle hand.

After all, my sisters and I were children taking care of children. All of us fought for a place in our sometimes loud, chaotic family. I was small and thin, a very shy, obedient, and quiet child. I oftentimes felt I was watching a huge drama unfold and wondered where I fit in.

Rebellion and anger were recurring behaviors of some of my siblings – all appropriate responses to the repression of feelings and lack of loving affirmation. After we turned five, I don't remember hearing our parents tell us they loved us. Years later, I read a definition of child emotional abuse: *withholding physical and emotional affection from a child.* But I could never say we weren't loved. We just had love of a different kind. It wasn't about expressing physical affection. We felt our parents' love and support in other ways. They were proud of our accomplishments, fed and clothed us, gave us a strong religious foundation, and encouraged our pursuits.

In the months that followed my diagnosis, I began 'to connect the dots,' discovering how my family rules may have well played a part in the formation of this disease. Not saying they caused it, but how I personally responded to things may well have caused an undo amount of stress that could then have contributed to this disease. I felt as if all I have ever believed about what's 'important' – especially work, producing and doing, was being challenged and changed.

Going through a box of old pictures and papers of my mother's, I came across a note from my kindergarten teacher, Mrs. Brown. She had written to my parents, '*Your little girl has been very friendly, cooperative and helpful even if she is rather shy and has a reserved nature. She loves praise and she likes to do little things to please us.* At a very early age, I had learned that *doing* was more important than *being*.

Low self-esteem, workaholic behavior and fear fueled my decisions. Prior to the diagnosis, I was aware I was a

27

workaholic, one whose self-esteem is based on what I produced. Deep down, I knew this way of living was not healthy or balanced. If I was not producing, then who was I? In graduate school, only an A was acceptable. In my work, perfection was the goal. Often, I stayed late to finish a project and skipped meals. I came to believe this frantic striving to be perfect, with the underlying message of *I don't measure up and someone will find out* contributed to the formation of this cancer. These messages depleted the energy I needed to function. Physiologically and emotionally, I was running on empty and making it easier for the cancer cells to take a foothold.

July 1995

"There is only one corner of the universe you can be certain of improving, and that is your own self. So you have to begin there, not outside, not on other people."
~Aldous Huxley

Not long after our meeting with Dr. Death, I re-read some notes from a retreat I attended fifteen years prior on the process of healing past hurts. At the beginning of his first talk, the retreat leader posed this question, "How do you know when you have healed from a hurt?" No one seemed to know the answer, so he went on to explain that when you see gifts come from the hurt, you know you are on a healing path. And so, as I began to see blessings from this crushing diagnosis, I knew that I was on the right path.

That month, Buzz and I attended the 25th wedding anniversary party of our dear friends, Dawn and Mike. A tent was pitched in their backyard. It was a soft, summer evening.

Everyone was in a joyous mood, laughing, joking, eating, and drinking, happy to be celebrating this wonderful milestone. "How are you?" friends would ask. I would reply, "Fine. How are you?" Concentrating on the words people were saying and responding without bursting into tears took tremendous energy. Everything seemed surreal. We did not share the 'cancer news,' as we wanted the evening to belong to our friends. I had written a blessing to be read before dinner in honor of my friend's milestone. Shortly after arriving I realized I would not be able to read it in this place filled with friends without crying. Luckily, her brother read it for me.

At dinner, I sat next to a relative of one of our friends. A nurse by profession, Kathleen was a quiet, gentle, compassionate soul. In a hushed voice, I found myself sharing with her this cancer secret. In a soft reassuring voice, she spoke of the great strides medicine was making in the curing of cancer, and yet, voiced her sadness that I had to travel this path. I was surprised I suddenly felt less frightened even a little lighter with her support and encouragement. She taught me a lesson about the power of compassionate listening – about being with and totally present to someone who was in a private hell.

Later, when Buzz and I returned home we made love, very tenderly, feeling as if we were alone drifting in a huge ocean of the unknown. Holding tight to each other there was an unspoken understanding that this moment was precious. How many more times would we be able to experience this intimate loving? Afterward, lying together holding each other, Buzz gently, placed his hands on my face and looked deeply into my eyes. Waiting a moment to gather his thoughts, he said, tenderly with heartfelt meaning "I want to ask your forgiveness for all the times I hurt you in our marriage, for all the times I made selfish decisions. Will you forgive me?" For the first time, I felt connected to his words and I knew he meant them. I could forgive him with a much deeper level of forgiveness, a blessing from this illness.

I began to do some serious soul searching, beginning with answering questions from Bernie Siegel's book, *Love, Medicine and Miracles.* As I peeled away my mask – that of the 'perfect Debbie,' the one I presented to the world, I felt fear grab me and I started to tremble. I was exposing myself. Was I a fraud? I took a deep breath and jumped feet first into my 'shadow' before I changed my mind. This dark part of me was hidden in my unconscious amidst fears about death and dying, fears about who I was, terrified I would find this person who never quite measured up.

Bernie Siegel asks difficult questions. "Why do you need your illness and what benefits do you derive from it?" It took a while to settle into this question. As with anything, we always skim over the top of things we don't want to face. We make excuses. Like I said, it took a while before I began to see. Squirming, I felt myself opening, exposing this 'long suffering' soul. Looking deep within, I did not recognize this person called 'me' who needed this illness to allow herself to take a health day, as illness is an acceptable reason for not going to work. I would not be seen as 'shirking my duties.' I needed my illness to perpetuate the role of 'martyr Debbie,' a role that brought me recognition during my husband's personal struggle with alcoholism: 'Look at Debbie, how long-suffering and courageous she is!'

There were times I wanted to throw the book away, but I continued. Another question Siegel asked, "What does the illness mean to you?" I didn't even hesitate with this one. I knew the answer. I felt labeled. People will never look at me the same way again. I felt less than perfect, flawed. My life would never be the same. Sad and grieved at the loss of my health, I wanted to believe this was a temporary loss, but I knew the threat would always be there, lurking in the shadows. Treatment terrified me. *What would chemotherapy be like? Would they find the cancer in my bone marrow?* On another level, I was aware that this was an opportunity to learn more life lessons. Bernie Siegel says, "Afflictions heal and adversity opens you to a new reality." I was on a wild roller coaster ride with my imagination and 'what ifs' were interspersed with an openness to learn.

Buzz and I continued to investigate holistic, alternative treatment protocols, however, we discovered very quickly these are not covered by insurance. Because of the severity of the diagnosis, we began to make appointments at major teaching hospitals to find an experimental treatment protocol. In the meantime, my priorities made a major shift. Hearing I had only five to seven years to live, my world stopped – and for the first time, I began to slow down enough to learn *how* I wanted to live. I wrote in my journal:

I will never take my life for granted again. I look at my children and family in a whole different way. I see their preciousness. My love for my husband deepens each day as we share our pain, thoughts and feelings. I am no longer in a hurry. I stop to consider the beauty in a flower. I talk to people, meditate, think, pray, cry, journal. I feel God's intense love for me in everyone and everything I see – friends, family, Nature, animals, the grace and blessing of our home. I see the beauty and preciousness of creation, God's gift to me.

One day, in one of these moments of pure gratitude, I flashbacked to the time Buzz and I were first married. As a young married couple with a small child, Buzz and I decided to move to Colorado. There was a job opportunity for him building homes in the mountains and we bought a condominium in Colorado Springs that overlooked Pikes Peak. Never having seen a mountain before, the Rocky Mountains were magnificent and soul moving. To me they were like God: solid, grounded, and immoveable. Years later, when I heard Thich Nhat Hanh, the beloved Buddhist monk, say, "Closing my eyes I see a mountain ... I am solid ..." I knew I could be like that mountain.

Never having lived away from home before, I began to miss my family and, surprisingly, I missed the black soil of Illinois. (Colorado Springs' soil is red and rocky.) After two years, we returned to Illinois. Moving in with my parents, our prayer became, "God, help us find a home that equals Pikes Peak in beauty." This was rather grandiose, since we had no money.

Several months later, Buzz was asked to repair a toilet at a rental property in St. Charles. In a side remark to Buzz, the owner said, "I am sick of this place. Why don't you buy it?" Buzz called me and I  came immediately. As I drove down the gravel lane, overgrown with vegetation, my heart raced. I rounded the curve in the lane and saw the small cottage style home in need of repair – but surrounded by mature trees, and I *knew* this was the answer to our prayer. Buzz's Dad loaned us the down payment and we moved in the following month.

The morning after we moved in, I awoke early and walked outside. It was an exquisite, warm, sweet-smelling, spring day in May with wild plum trees in full bloom. Navigating through a jumble of tall grasses, I made my way through the backyard and stumbled over a large, round,

32

concrete foundation filled with weeds and native flowers. I later discovered this was the silo of the farm that had been on the land here years ago. Sitting down, I breathed in the beauty around me, praying, and thanking God for answering our prayer, when a huge bull snake crawled in front of me. Normally, I would have screamed and run in the house, however, my heart was filled with gratitude and my senses were saturated with the splendor of that spring day. This was a 'Kairos' moment, a God moment. So, what would the symbol of a snake mean? I thought about the snake in the shedding of skin being an ancient symbol for re-birth. I did not realize then that on this little piece of earth, I would slowly be re-born, shedding the dead skin of negative thinking and behaviors that do not serve life.

This house and property – this piece of earth – belongs to us for only a short time, as life spans are short in the scheme of creation. Along with the happiness, there would be sadness and struggle. I accepted this truth with a glad heart and knew God would be my solace and rock like the heavy boulders strewn about the property.

So now, twenty-five years later, I was right in the middle of the sadness and struggle I had predicted. We knew I must find an experimental protocol at a large teaching hospital, to go along with conventional chemotherapy. The three major teaching hospitals in Chicago I was considering for treatment requested a CAT scan to determine the stage of the lymphoma. On a scale of one to four, four was the most aggressive stage.

On the day of the test, my heart was beating wildly as I was placed on a long table that would be sent incrementally into a thick, arched canopy. *What would they find?*

"Breathe," I kept saying to calm myself. I closed my eyes as the machine took me into the darkened arch. As the machine lurched forward, I remembered a book called *Mary, The Womb of God* that I had borrowed from my mother several years before the diagnosis. Focusing on the word, 'womb' I instantly pictured myself in the 'womb' of God. I felt calm and safe.

The results of the CAT scan found an enlarged node above my kidney. With nodes above and below my diaphragm, I was diagnosed with Stage 2, out of 4, and I would definitely need chemotherapy to attack the cancer systemically.

In the days that followed, I began to re-discover my senses, to *quiet* myself, to *look* at and *listen* to my world. Peter London said it well: "A quieted mind within a body at peace prepares us for perceiving that portion of the talking universe (Nature) that speaks softly and at a pace beneath and beyond that of ordinary consciousness." I slowly began to experience the 'talking universe' where I found a 'home' for what was raging inside me. One day, this 'talking universe' appeared in a very unexpected way.

Having scheduled an appointment to see an oncologist at Northwestern in Chicago, I decided to spend some time at Lake Michigan. I was worried about being around my large, lively, extended  family on this weekend at the lake while in this sad, shocked state. Before I left, Buzz suggested that I picture a pink cloud above my head, instead of a dark stormy one. For the first day or two I stoically held in my fear and grief. Many times, I wanted to cry hysterically or scream some profanity.

On the third day, a sudden storm blew in while we were at the beach. Quickly, clouds, darkness, and a strong wind enveloped us. A storm without lightening was quickly upon us. It was as if the storm mirrored my interior being.

Without thought, I suddenly ran into the lake and began to swim in the turbulent water, as if, somehow, I could rid myself of the terror of this living nightmare. I swam as if someone was chasing me, and, at the same time, reveled in the power and beauty of Nature. When I could swim no more, exhausted, I crawled out of the lake. The storm passed as quickly as it came and the sun returned with a soft breeze. Sitting on the beach, wrapped in a wet towel, I saw my life as a huge, terrifying drama that was slowly unfolding. A part of me wanted the drama to quickly unfold to my death, feeling that I had no control over my destiny. What was the point of fighting? In front of me, I watched the children playing industriously in the sand, digging a hopeless hole with a wall around it that kept caving in with each wave. Evan, my six-year-old nephew, kept digging out the sand and never gave up. Watching him, I began to laugh. A six-year-old child was telling me to change my attitude – an attitude I decided to adopt.

On that day at the beach, I experienced Nature as a 'container.' I could not contain the feelings that were storming inside of me, and Nature provided a perfect opportunity to help me. As I swam and battled the waves and experienced the awesome strength of Nature, the fear and terror subsided. In the months ahead, the waves of fear would arise and then fall. I would 'battle' to be healed and surprised to see that the strength and power in Nature was also in me.

Still working as a therapist at the addiction-counseling center I wondered what decision to make about working. In graduate school, I had decided that my goal was to become a Licensed Clinical Social Worker so I could develop a private practice. I was wisely advised by Abby, who was already eleven years into the same field, to develop a strong knowledge of addictions, since in private practice I would encounter addictions of every kind. She was right.

At the age of forty-eight, I had already witnessed the pain and frustration of the effects of alcoholism in my family, my friends and in my own marriage. Being the spouse of a recovering alcoholic, I had to face my own addiction to co-dependent behavior, discovering that my peace and happiness were dependent on the emotional state and behaviors of others. If my husband was happy, I was happy. If he was angry, I became threatened and frustrated and intrusively tried to fix it, then becoming angry if he did not follow my advice.

One day, years before I became ill, I discovered my husband was drinking, after he had told me he quit. Rage, fueled by fear and helplessness, spilled out of my mouth. I found myself screaming at Buzz, "You are a fucking loser!" I had become someone I did not like.

The next day, I called a therapist knowledgeable in addictions and began the long process of healing. Paula was about my age, with a vast knowledge of addictions. She told me it was mandatory that I attend Al-Anon and start reading material that would help me understand alcoholism as a family disease. What relief to hear Paula say to me, "You did not cause it, you cannot cure it and you cannot control it. You can only take care of yourself and own the part of you that was enabling Buzz to drink." Al-Anon helped me to lovingly detach from Buzz's behavior and focus on what I needed. And, when I focused on what I needed, my husband also began to heal.

I also kept asking myself, "When and how do I share this cancer news with my clients? Can I be an effective therapist in the midst of all of this?" I prayed and asked God, "Where are you taking me, Lord? Where do I need to be? What is best for me?"

I finally shared the news about my illness with my clients in the Thursday therapy group, and felt as if a tremendous burden had lifted. The group was concerned and compassionate. Going home that day, I felt lighter and more peaceful. I had actually experienced a 'normal' day and even enjoyed the day. After work, I had shared my news with co-workers, Trish and Linda. Linda gave me some of her precious stones, ones she felt had healing properties. Two of them were smooth, green, malachite stones, one white quartz, and a pair of earrings with 'healing stones.' She also gave me her most valued stone in a little, soft-leather bag, telling me to sleep with it under my pillow. I was profoundly touched by her love and concern. I thought, it doesn't really matter whether one believes in the healing power of stones, I felt the love of God in these stones, for God made them and they were given in love. Linda hugged me and we cried together.

I shared the cancer diagnosis with my Tuesday therapy group and two people cried. I was touched. I was observing that the mention of cancer put people into a state of instant fear. This did not surprise me, as having cancer was one of my worst fears. One client, who had experienced physical and emotional abandonment as a child by his father and later in life – a divorce, used an incident in group to become angry with me, so I would become angry with him. He could then 'righteously' write me off, so he would not have to face another loss. I would not play his game and calmly responded to his outburst. Later, we talked about what happened.

For two days, I felt almost normal and then heavy again. I was beginning to feel the pressure of making a decision about choosing a treatment. The downside of 'slow-growing,' non-Hodgkin's lymphoma is that there was no cure and it kept coming back. The upside is that the cells divide and grow slowly, therefore, I had a little more time to make up my mind about treatment.

Anxious and scared, I called together my sisters and some women friends to meet once a week to share and pray together for healing and discernment. Twenty years prior to the cancer diagnosis, while I struggled with motherhood and marriage, a group of my friends and sisters met every week for three years to share and pray about our human and spiritual journeys. We came from all different religious traditions.

I was raised in a very traditional Catholic home. My maternal ancestry (German, with some Scotch/Irish) and paternal ancestry (all German) were deeply rooted in the Catholic faith. Braving the perils of crossing the ocean, of leaving their homes and family, my great-grandparents on both sides came with the great immigration wave of the 1890's to the United States. It was their faith in God, taught to them through the Catholic Church that sustained them. This strong faith and loyalty to the church was passed on to my parents who tried to instill the same teachings to my siblings and myself.

We attended church on Sunday and every day that the church deemed *Holy*. For my parents, this was no small feat to corral and herd ten children into a church pew on time! Christmas and Easter were huge celebrations. As children, not only did we participate in the secular activities such as the Easter Bunny and Santa Claus, we were also immersed in the rituals of the church and the lives of the Saints that set the foundation for the mysterious, the miraculous, and the mystical – a fertile soil for my faith to grow.

For example, every Easter Holy Week, my mother would insist my siblings and I attend church sometime between noon and three in the afternoon on Good Friday and say the Stations of the Cross. My memories of those times are vivid – the sharp smell of incense burning in a candle lit, darkened church. The people, us included, quietly and reverently standing in front of each station, a picture – fourteen in all – placed along the walls of the church, each portraying the passion of Christ. We would silently pray, then move to the next station while trying to imagine the way of the cross, Jesus scourged and whipped, Jesus standing before Pilate; Jesus falling the first, second and third time, Jesus nailed to the cross, and so on. A sacred sense of the holiness of this day permeated the sanctuary. I often felt tearful, as I pictured Jesus walking the Via Dolorosa in Rome on his way to be crucified. Even as a child, I would ponder over and over the question – *how could He love me that much?* And in my teens, *what is this unconditional love of God?*

Not only did we attend church on Sundays, every Thursday afternoon in the town where I grew up, whether you were Catholic or Protestant, we were released from school early to attend 'church school.' On Sundays, after Mass we were expected to attend class to learn more about Catholicism through an excruciating, boring book called the Baltimore Catechism. We were expected to memorize the answers to questions like 'what is a sacrament?' We would all parrot, "A sacrament is an outward sign instituted by God to give grace."

Passing on the Catholic teachings was a serious priority for my parents, which was brought home to me one Sunday, while attending a fourth-grade religious education class. Much to my shock and disbelief, the teacher ordered me out of the classroom.

"Debbie, I am surprised at your behavior. I have asked you several times not to talk during the times I am teaching. Please leave the room and wait in the next room until class is over."

Even I was surprised at my behavior, the perfect pupil, who was usually obedient, quiet and shy. Horrified and humiliated, with my head bowed, I left the classroom and sat at a school desk in the cold, empty room. Thinking about having to face the teacher and my classmates again, an inspired thought came to me. *Class is almost over. I will walk home and tell my parents class was let out early.*

The mile walk home was cold and lonely, across the Fox River bridge that connected the east and west side of town, and past the hills behind the large A&P grocery store where we would go to sled, when there was enough snow.

My plan was to quietly open the front door and slip into the house unnoticed. However, the thick, massive, oak door slipped out of my hand and slammed shut. The loud voice of my Dad came from the fireplace room.

"Who is it?"

The house seemed unusually quiet. Suddenly, it dawned on me everyone was still at religious education class.

"It's me, Deb."

As I stood before him in his favorite red, wing back chair, the logs in the fireplace crackled and spit embers on the stone hearth.

Putting the newspaper down, he asked,

"Why are you home so early from catechism class?"

With my heart pounding, I stammered, "Class was let out early."

"Then why isn't anyone else home?" he demanded to know.

I was caught dead in my lie and had to come clean. He was furious.

"Don't you *ever* misbehave in that class again. I will tan your hide from top to bottom. The very idea that you gave the teacher grief when she was trying to teach you something important – and she doesn't even get paid!" He went on yelling, "If you ever lie to me again, you will not see the light of day for a month of Sundays!"

Growing up, there was a lot of teaching about how much God loved us, however, there were also many rules about behavior and what would happen to you if these rules were broken – the possibility of an eternity of hell and damnation. As children, we would evaluate constantly whether our behavior was a mortal sin, which was a really big sin – like missing church on Sunday or a venial sin like talking back to your parents or lying. We were told that if you died with a mortal sin on your soul the destination would be hell, an eternity of suffering.

To this day, I feel a little guilty when I don't go to church on Sundays. So, I would say, absolutely, I was taught to fear God. My parents, the church, and society used this fear of damnation to keep everyone in check. Many Christian churches still bastardize the teachings of Christ. They preach about the infinite love of God and then switch to the eternal fires of hell if one falls out of grace. What a horrible, cruel way to teach children about God! How can anyone love or trust such a God? Fortunately, there were many wise spiritual teachers in the world that taught about the infinite love of God and I was lucky enough to find them. Paradoxically, my fear of God motivated me to seek and question what I was taught as a child!

As a child and young teen, I sometimes whined and complained about going to church. For the most part, I did not mind church; I was too afraid of going to hell. It was a chance to dress up, especially on Christmas and Easter. There was a family cohesiveness and a sense that this activity was gravely important. So important, that after attending public grade school, my parents sent me and most of my siblings to

Catholic high schools. They were intent on all of us developing a strong faith in God and more importantly, getting into heaven and the only way they could see how to do this was through the Catholic Church. All you had to do was to go to church and obey the rules of the Church laid down by your parish priest. As a young teen, I began to see that it was not so simple.

One hot, summer day toward evening, after dinner, I sat down on the front porch stoop. Closing my eyes and resting my head on the porch pillar behind me, I relished the cool evening breeze. Soon, the front door opened and Dad quietly sat down on the opposite side of the long step. He, too, was silent – taking in the sweet, cool summer air. This was a side of my father I rarely saw. He was always moving, working, and doing.

Before Dad joined me, I had been thinking about my maternal grandparents who were still alive and living in Springfield, Illinois, where both my parents grew up. A little uncomfortable with the silence and curious to know more about my paternal grandmother who was deceased, I asked, "Dad, what happened to your Mother? How old were you when she died?" (Dad was the youngest of nine children.) Dad's face softened and in a sad, quiet voice, looking out into the distance, he shared a few details of what happened.

"Mom was walking to the store and a car hit her. An ambulance took her to the hospital. She was there for several weeks. I was only twelve years old."

Horrified, I could not imagine the death of one of my parents at such a young age.

"That is terrible, Dad."

With an angry edge to his voice, he added, "Every night, I prayed to God that she would be all right. But she

42

died." He then added bitterly, "No child should be without a parent."

After a few moments, wordlessly, Dad got up and went into the house.

That conversation stayed with me, and years later it suddenly occurred to me why it was so important to Dad that we welcomed foster children into our home. After losing his mother, he could not bear the thought of a homeless child. Mom was not as invested in this idea; after all, our home was already bursting with the eight of us. Dad would say, "Corinne, what is one more child? They have no place to go."

Mom finally agreed. Bill and Frances stayed for twelve years and a parade of other foster children stayed for short periods of time until foster homes could be found for them. Because of our parents' example, all of us, through the years, have become compassionate givers.

In my short conversation with Dad that night on the front porch, the desolation and grief of the senseless death of his mother spoke volumes, and the disappointment and hurt that God did not answer a little boy's prayer. I was learning, bad things happen to good people, but Dad kept going to church with his unanswered questions and insisting his children do the same.

Whereas, Mom and Dad were in total agreement their children receive a religious foundation, Mom became an example to me as she questioned the patriarchal Catholic Church, the rules about contraception and the little recognition women received in the Church. As I moved through my teen years to college and married life with small children, I absolutely drew upon the theological underpinnings I received from the Catholic Church. But I also questioned the Church's teachings and, like my mother, began a search of my own to develop a personal relationship with God. I discovered that one can have all the knowledge in the world of scripture and theology, but until there is an experience of God, it is all meaningless.

Over the years, prior to the cancer diagnosis, I did have many of those sacramental, experiential moments. Shortly after I was married, my mother called me and said that I *must* attend a 'prayer meeting' at the Church on Wednesday night. She said, "If you go, it will change your life." I could not imagine anything so foreign, yet I went because over the past several months there was a voice inside me that kept saying over and over *there must be more to God than church on Sunday!* What I encountered that evening was part of a movement that was sweeping the Catholic Church and was soon known as the Catholic Charismatic Movement. I was stunned by the joy, peace and excitement about God that seemed to permeate the room. With Mom playing the piano, there was singing, spontaneous vocal prayer, 'hands-on' praying for healing, and everyone was carrying a Bible and talking about having a 'personal relationship with God.' I didn't understand it all, but I knew I wanted what they had.

Slowly, seeking God through studying the Bible for the first time, going to retreats, meeting with other women who had similar questions about God and faith, praying and reading spiritual books, the denominational walls I was taught as a child – that Catholicism was the only way to God came crashing down. In my seeking, I was discovering and experiencing with aha moments the love of God for others and me. Discovering that God's love is inclusive not exclusive to only Catholics, the beauty and gifts of all spiritualties became apparent to me.

These aha moments gave me strength and the motivation to keep searching for God. What I did not realize was the extent my life was driven by fear which almost annihilated and certainly kept in the shadows my experiences of God up to that time – making it impossible for me to have a deep, emotional, lasting connection with God. I was soon to discover that the chains of fear are insidious and can wrap very tightly around you unless you are mindful and conscious of their strength and power to spiral you into a vortex of negativity and darkness.

In the course of the cancer journey, it was now time to call back the 'prayer warriors,' from the past. They all said they would meet and walk with me on this cancer journey. Meeting together, we shared, prayed, and cried together, asking God to give me direction in choosing an oncologist.

No matter all the love and support I had from family and friends, I soon discovered I was alone on the journey. Having cancer, there are many decisions to make – life and death decisions! The questions: Do I follow all the recommendations of my Western trained doctors? What alternative treatments might help? Can I do both? Where do I go for treatment? I had to make these decisions alone – doing what was best for me, whatever that was. In the past, one of my sisters had been frustrated with me because I grind over making decisions. Often, I have blamed my difficulty in making personal decisions on my Libra birth. In 'balancing the scales,' I see both sides clearly, so, which way is best? Or perhaps, I was used to having others in my life make the decisions for me. There was no place to turn now. This one was on me.

All the great spiritual masters say we face God alone. We are all responsible as to how we respond to life and the decisions we have made. I asked God to help guide me with these decisions and slowly I began to see God's hand in this painful place. I started to listen to that intuitive knowing, and sometimes just took a deep breath and made a decision, trusting all would be well. The blessing for me was a deepening of my sense of personal power and owning my connection to the divine. It was as if God was waiting for me all these years to finally acknowledge the divine goodness and strength in me.

Sleeping was becoming a challenge. One night I awoke to moonlight streaming into my window, spreading a golden light across the foot of the bed. I crawled down into the light and was suddenly struck by how much I didn't know about the universe. Bathing in the moon glow and soaking in its beauty and light, it felt as if the moon was absorbing my fear. The moonlight became another 'container.' Looking at the moon, I became deeply aware of how much I did not know about creation and myself. A deeper desire to seek truth stirred in me.

Several days later, I ran into Helen, a very traditional Catholic friend who gave me a beautiful holy card with a prayer to say *every day*. I was struck by the loving gestures of people. I gratefully accepted them all for I knew I felt God's love through them. I remembered a retreat I once attended with a friend where the participants were asked to stand in a circle and hold hands and then, very gently explore the hand we were holding with our eyes closed. The leader then said, "The hand you are holding is the hand of God. Who are God's hands, but ours?" That knowledge brought me moments of peace and consolation.

With all of these decisions to make it was becoming clear – I needed Laurie more now than ever. She was my advocate since the beginning, and I trusted her insight. She blessed me with her scientific mind, compassionate heart and tenacity in getting the information needed.

After weeks of phone calls and research, Buzz, who was trying to keep finances and family together while dealing with the possibility I might die and he being thrown into single parenthood, was operating in a hyper-state of family survival. Being self-employed, he threw himself into his business. We were awakening to the realization that insurance would cover some, but not all, of my treatment, especially not any alternative treatments.

How will we manage financially? I couldn't stop wondering how this would all turn out.

The slide pathology, so far, was sent to my local hospital and three major teaching hospitals. The type of lymphoma determines the treatment, but there was still no agreement as to whether I had 'slow-growing' or 'intermediate' non-Hodgkin's lymphoma. This not knowing became almost unbearable. Desiring that I have the freedom to decide my choice of treatment, Chaitan, Buzz's sister's husband, and being a wonderful doctor specializing in Immunology and Nuclear Medicine Cancer Research at Sloan Kettering, gently recommended Northwestern Hospital. The oncologist from Northwestern was kind and gave us time. In a gentle voice, he said at this point in time there was no cure for slow-growing lymphoma; however, he was excited about a new drug called Rituxan, which was still in the experimental stage. He was hopeful that I might qualify as a candidate for the last experimental protocol.

August 1995

*"Stay with me God, the night is dark, the night
is cold: my little spark of courage dies. The night is long.
Be with me God ..."*
~Anonymous Soldier

As I juggled working, family, cancer treatment decisions and the prospect of dying, my head was swimming with wild thoughts and emotions. Joe, the director of the addiction counseling center where I worked, suggested I see a woman who was formerly a nurse, and now a psychotherapist trained to work with cancer patients. Dr. Nancy was gentle, kind and patient with her empathic understanding for this 'adjustment disorder,' a mental health diagnosis given to people who have experienced a traumatic event that disrupts their ability to function normally, often accompanied with depression and anxiety. Being free to unload all my fears and tears with her gave me a foundation, a solid footing, so that I could move forward with important decisions. Her suggestions were extremely important and she gave me a course of action for the path I needed to take to support my healing. With her guidance, I did not feel as impotent and helpless.

Sitting back on the couch, she suggested I use imagery to help the medicine do its job. She went on to give me examples and educated me on the positive effect this would have on my treatment and the healing of this disease. After some thought, I decided to use a non-violent imagery of ladybugs eating aphids, aka the cancer cells. Aphids are little insects that injure roses and other flowers and are a delicious food for ladybugs. Even though I did not begin chemotherapy until September, I began immediately to engage the imagery every day. My own research had also endorsed the positive effects of implementing creative imagery.

Next, Dr. Nancy took me through a guided imagery helping me create a safe place in my mind, with the suggestion that I visit this place whenever I felt fearful and immobilized. To this day, I can 'see' my safe place, a large room filled with windows looking out over a lovely vista of rolling hills and trees. There is a crackling fire in the stone fireplace with a soft comfortable couch in front of the protective hearth; flower arrangements and beautiful artwork decorate the room. During the guided imagery, she had asked me if I wanted anyone present with me in the room, and I immediately thought of Jesus. Whenever I wished, I could summon the presence of Jesus to sit with me in this beautiful space and be with me, holding me, if necessary.

Her third suggestion surprised me, however, it made a tremendous difference to my fearful attitude toward chemotherapy. Very emphatically she said, "Look at chemotherapy as an ally, not as an evil. Make friends with chemotherapy, so you can help it do its job of killing cancer cells." Looking at chemotherapy as an ally was not easy, especially in the months to come, but I was able to slowly change my attitude, which helped alleviate the stress and fear in taking chemotherapy drugs.

Then looking intently, her finger pointing at me and with a slightly raised voice stressing the importance of her words, knowing these words could mean life or death for me, she said, "Set aside time each day to rest and engage the positive imagery. It is time for you to dump the guilt about not producing, and to take the time you need to heal." Hearing these words was like having warm oil poured over a wound. I was actually given permission to put myself first, to focus on taking whatever time I needed to heal. In fact, it was more like an order, with dire consequences if I did not follow through. Gratitude and relief flowed through me. Lastly, Dr. Nancy affirmed the importance of journaling to help me uncover any unconscious motivation for the appearance of this cancer, to recognize the gift in this painful place and to create a space to express the whirling thoughts and emotions that took over my brain.

Upon returning home that day, I explained to Buzz and the children that I needed quiet time each day to focus on practicing guided imagery or to listen to meditation tapes to help me stay focused and positive about treatment, and that I would put a 'Do Not Disturb' sign on my bedroom door for thirty minutes each day. This was a difficult decision. In the past, I was always available to everyone at any time.

Several weeks into psychotherapy, I began to have disturbing thoughts about the illness, about being put center stage and bringing me attention I never received as a child. I was stunned at the outpouring of love and support from family, friends and people I did not even know. I began having these awful thoughts of being healed and losing my 'sick status.' Those were terrifying thoughts. I knew nothing remains hidden. My body would 'hear' these thoughts and not be healed.

One day toward the end of a session, feeling ashamed and silly, I haltingly told her about these thoughts.

She empathically responded, "What is important is that you told someone. Keeping those thoughts inside is what gives them power. We will turn this around and instead of you being the Poor Sick One, you will be the *Star of Recovery*." I let out a deep breath of relief. She was not shocked or surprised at my response to being ill.

As I soaked in her words, *Star of Recovery,* I felt an instant positive shift in my outlook toward this disease.

Early in our sessions, Dr. Nancy encouraged me to write down my dreams. "Oftentimes," she said, "dreams become more vivid and lucid when you begin psychotherapy. It's as if your unconscious gets the message you are serious about looking deeper." Pushing her blonde hair off her face, she continued, "Everyone dreams. If you want to remember your dreams, then tell your unconscious. Place a notebook by your bed and upon waking, with gentle, soft movements reach for it and write the words that come to mind, for example, *desert*, *Mom*, *falling*, *snake*, and such to keep the dream from slipping away."

In my reading, I learned dreams, as gifts from our unconscious, use symbols from the conscious world to guide us towards our personal growth and healing. They can be their own little 'prairie burn' to purify and cleanse by bringing to light toxic thoughts, attitudes and behaviors that are harmful and eat away at our souls. Dreams always come in the service of health and healing.

I began to remember my dreams, which were sometimes frightening, but always healing and life giving. I experienced this dream when I made the decision to seek professional help:

I was watching Elvis perform onstage, from the side close to where he changed outfits. I had on a skimpy top that kept falling open, so I wanted to borrow one of his tops. In the next scene I was in a messy kitchen. Elvis came down looking for a glass of water. I realized, much to my horror, I had bed-head. He looked interested in me because of the skimpy top. I ran off to a swimming pool to dunk my head in water, but I could not find access to the pool. I was frustrated and wanted to return to Elvis, although I knew I would be another 'toy' to him. I was tired and finally lay down in the grass.

When I woke up I listed the important words, looking at them symbolically to see if there were any healing connections for me.

Dream Thoughts:

Looking good has been very important to me. I have often felt the need to attract the admiration and acceptance of both sexes. I asked myself if my intention was to look good for love of self or, was I seeking the attention and acceptance I never received as a child? I decided it was the latter.

- Messy kitchen is symbolic of my body, mind, and spirit at the moment and before the cancer diagnosis. I wondered what 'messy food for thought' I was feeding my mind and spirit. The kitchen is also a creative space. What is it I am re-creating in myself?
- Elvis is a symbol of fame, the 'ultimate prize' for many women. If the 'King' finds me desirable, I must be!
- Bed-head is symbolic of being messed up, flawed, and unacceptable. If my hair is messed up, then I am all of that. That belief *is* a messed-up head!
- Water is symbolic of becoming conscious. In the dream, I only wanted to use the water to be rid of the shame and embarrassment of having a bed-head. The dream would not let me near the water, as if to say, 'getting rid of bed-head will not heal the woundedness in you that says you must look good to be enough.'

Even though I knew Elvis' attraction was purely physical, there was a part of me that would prostitute myself for his short-lived acceptance. Therefore, I supported my self-esteem by what other people said about me and whether they found me physically attractive. I was exhausted by always trying to look good. I knew then this did not serve my soul. In the dream I laid down in the grass to rest. The cancer had forced me to rest. In the dream, I remember saying to myself, *I am ready to rest.*

With a spirit of openness to understand my body, mind and spirit connection, I prayed for other sources of information to help. A friend gave me Ann Frahm's book, *Cancer Battle Plan*. It helped immensely to shift my attitude of helplessness to an attitude of empowerment. Every day, I asked myself what can I do to take charge of my fight for health? I would then make my list. Today I will:

- ✓ drink green tea
- ✓ take vitamins
- ✓ exercise
- ✓ find a nutritionist
- ✓ make an appointment with another oncologist
- ✓ set a date for the next gathering of women to pray
- ✓ meditate

While checking off my completed tasks each day, I would say to myself, 'I will be a victor today.' I felt more empowered taking charge of my life and my health. Focusing on my needs continued to feel uncomfortable. Radical change in diet, cultivating a meditation practice as a discipline and exercise, were never the norm for me. Perhaps illness would have been the only way I would have taken the time to incorporate these important practices. Maybe, just maybe, the 'stubbornness' of this indolent, slow-growing lymphoma was a metaphor for my stubbornness in taking care of myself.

I was looking at all the 'Big Guns' in many of the teaching hospitals in Chicago. In my continuing search for an oncologist, another doctor was highly recommended to me, a woman oncologist.

When we met, she explained her treatment of choice was an aggressive protocol using Interferon, a cancer drug, along with a bone marrow transplant. This treatment had promise, especially with those patients with a 'bulky' presentation of cancer. Although mine was found above and below my diaphragm, this did not necessarily qualify as bulky or advanced. Another marker to qualify me for this treatment would be whether the cancer was in my bone marrow and, to determine this, I needed a bone marrow biopsy, which would determine the severity of this cancer diagnosis. They warned me of how excruciatingly painful this test could be, if not done correctly.

Extremely nervous about the possible painful procedure, I was surprised how well the procedure went. While lying on my side, a huge fat needle was injected into my back to collect the bone marrow. With the pain medicine, it was not as horrible as I had imagined. Now we needed to wait.

While waiting over the weekend for results we attended an Italian wedding in New York City. It was one of the most memorable weddings we ever attended. The reception room was huge with a large table at the entrance filled with a variety of delicious appetizers with an ice sculpture in the middle. There was a large dance floor with tables all around the floor. In the front of the room was a stage decorated on each side with enormous floral arrangements. In the middle of the meal, dancers came out in Las Vegas type costumes, entertaining everyone. After the filet mignon dinner, another table held a variety of French desserts with a water fountain and flowers in the center. Shortly after dinner, the dance band began to play Motown music and everybody danced. After several hours of dancing, another table was laden with coffee, tea, drinks and a variety of fruits and cheeses. The whole evening was orchestrated beautifully. There were no long, boring speeches, no long stretches of time waiting for the bride to cut the cake or throw her bouquet. For one wonderful evening, the word *cancer* barely entered my mind. What a welcome relief.

Back home, I was face to face with the treatment issue. No one seemed to have a definitive answer for me. We were scheduled to see one more doctor at another teaching hospital, with more information to consider. I needed to make a decision soon. I kept praying God would give me wisdom to know which path to take.

"Breathe," I said to myself over and over. I wanted to focus on each day and all that it held for me. I whispered, "How can I be a victor today and not a victim? I will list my blessings."

- I thank God today for Buzz. I felt such a wave of love for him this morning while he was sleeping.
- For my beautiful children.
- For Laurie for her tenacious attitude in finding the best way to go in choosing a treatment protocol.
- For my family and friends for the 'protective cover' I feel today, which must be their prayers and loving concern.

Several days later I received a phone call from the doctor's office telling me my bone marrow was *clean*. A languid and warm feeling moved through my body like wading through a rain puddle resting in the summer sun. Breathing deeply, I closed my eyes and thanked the nurse.

The weeks passed. I still hadn't decided which experimental protocol to choose for treatment. Do I choose the protocol from Northwestern? Or do I choose a more aggressive but promising protocol? Based on the biopsy slides, five leading university hospitals could not agree on the type of lymphoma I had and each offered different treatment options. Chaitan said in a gentle way, "Proceed one step at a time. Let the hospitals battle it out." I felt blessed to have his counsel. He was very patient and sensitive about not imposing his hospital preference and choice of treatment. Non-Hodgkin's lymphoma was not his expertise and he wanted me to cover all possibilities before I made my treatment decision.

The choice was mine to make. And mine alone.

Our final doctor interview was with an oncologist from a major teaching hospital who was continually referenced in the cancer studies Laurie was researching. Excited and hopeful, we made an appointment and sent all my slide pathology and impressions from the other hospitals.

At the appointment, Laurie and I were shown into a large consultation room without windows. Full of anticipation, while waiting for the doctor, we went over the questions we wanted to ask. Soon a middle aged, slender man swept into the room with an entourage of interns. He briefly shook our hands and introduced himself, speaking in a professor-like, assertive and dispassionate voice:

"I have reviewed your slides and information. I can give you chemotherapy. I can give you antibodies, Interferon, anything you want, but there is no cure for the type of cancer you have."

Laurie and I were speechless.

Sounding to us like the ultimate salesman, not caring about me, only about the sale of another possible number for scientific research. There was no connection with this doctor. There was no excitement in his voice about any treatment protocol. For me there was not enough healing energy, hope or compassion emanating from the heart of this man.

No Sale. I remembered from my reading it is critically important for patients to connect with and trust their oncologist. I would *not* put my life in the hands of someone who believed there was no hope of healing.

Once upon a time, before cancer, I was bored with normal. Now, I would give anything to experience normal. What a roller-coaster ride! The bills kept pouring in. We were constantly worrying if our insurance would pay. Overwhelmed with work and dealing with this disease, my mind whirled as I asked myself over and over what to do with work. *Should I work less? Should I take a leave of absence? Should I just quit?* I needed to get away.

Mom understood the importance of a spiritual connection and made it financially possible for me to attend retreats at the nearby Cenacle Retreat House which we had been going to for many years. The Cenacle Sisters opened their arms to all faiths. It was a safe, quiet place enveloped by the beauty of Nature. Looking back now, these retreats, had always brought meaning, focus, and healing which gave me the strength and spiritual courage to navigate the uncharted waters of this cancer journey.

I have always considered the Cenacle an old friend, having experienced twenty years of going there for renewal and healing and yet, this time, walking into the chapel was sad and painful. Everywhere I went for the first time after receiving this dreadful diagnosis was painful. Being told of an illness is like a death. The part that was healthy had died. I was now in a different category. One of the sick.

I did not feel betrayed or angry with God. As I looked at my lifestyle, I thought, 'Why not me?' With every death there is a re-birth and I knew I was in the gestation period. I was stuck in the middle, holding both life and death. Eckhart Tolle says there is no such thing as *life and death*, only *life and re-birth*.

God's presence was very real on that first evening at the Cenacle. I kept hearing the same message of God's energy and love in the universe, in Nature, in people.

After the evening session, I went outside and sat alone on the front porch. I felt a soft, moist, cool wind blowing through the trees, which were silhouetted against a pale gray sky. Dancing in the wind, the tops of the tall trees looked as if they were waving to me and having a wonderful time. *I could hear them whispering. Did they know of my illness?* I began to talk to my body, telling her that she needed to get rid of this cancer. Fighting 'looking ridiculous,' I walked over to a tree  and wrapped my arms around it, soaking in its strength and solid, healthy presence, which was full of energy and life. Quietly, I asked the tree for some of its energy to help me heal my body.

On my walk the next morning, I hugged another tree. I decided then and there I was an official 'tree hugger.' My love affair with trees began that weekend. As I hugged the tree, I felt a gentle 'give' of its large trunk as the wind blew through the branches; yet, I sensed the strength and groundedness of the tree. Once again, Nature gave me a container to hold me and I became like that tree – strong and solid to make the difficult decisions that not only would save my life, but would also give me new life.

Feeling warm and protected in this loving Cenacle space, my thoughts began to wander. The desire to stay at home for a period of rest and regrouping was beginning to sound more and more like a good idea. As a workaholic, my self-esteem was tightly woven into what I produced. I wondered, do I have the courage to let go of my work?

The topic for the weekend was about St. Teresa of Avila and her book *The Interior Castle*. Over the weekend, I fell in love with this Saint. How well she described the different 'dwelling places' in the journey of spiritual growth. I was relieved to see one can float back and forth between the different dwelling places, and that they are not to be used to measure your spiritual maturity. Teresa says, "God gives what God pleases when God pleases." I came away with a stronger resolve to focus on spiritual growth. I wrote in my journal:

My path is set. I will move toward the center dwelling place. I cannot stop my movement to God. I am forever drawn. At times, I am frightened for I fear more suffering. Do I need to suffer to grow?

Teresa says,

"Let nothing trouble you.
Let nothing frighten you.
All things pass away.
God never changes.
Patience obtains all things.
God alone suffices."

Teresa's words became my mantra for the next seven months. Shortly after this retreat, I experienced another dream that helped me make a decision about my job. In my dream,

I was late for a train. My friends were also running for the train. I started to follow them, but I could not run because my shoes were on the wrong feet. I switched the shoes and took off running, bumping into people. Losing track of my friends, I could not find the train.

Waking up from the dream, exhausted and out of breath, I focused on the themes of *being late, unprepared,* and *left behind.* The train symbolized transportation, getting from one place to another. I could not even transport myself because my shoes were on the wrong feet. Where did I want to go? Immediately, my inner voice responded, *I want to go to a place of health.* Therefore, I reasoned, 'What changes must I make to walk 'right' and to arrive at a healthy, healed place?' First, I needed to get my 'shoes on the right feet' by thinking about what I needed to heal and to stop taking care of everyone else. Because of this dream, and what was surfacing at the very core of my being, truth was rising to the top, and it was crystal clear. I would miss the train of life if I did not make some changes.

Several weeks later I applied for an extended leave of absence from work. I had many sleepless nights as I tossed and turned going over and over my fear of having no money. I remembered a time as a young teen. In his attempt to encourage parents of his parish to send their girls to a Catholic high school, which was ten miles away, our parish priest, Monsignor Donovan, gave each girl bus money for the month. Toward the middle of one month, I had spent my bus money on lipstick and makeup. In the morning, before going to the bus stop, I nervously approached Dad for money. He screamed at me, "What the god damn hell did you do with your bus money?" I sheepishly shrugged my shoulders. He slammed the money on the table. It was painful for him to part with money. He was not interested in my desire to look pretty as an adolescent girl trying to fit in. I sensed his fear of being without money, his fear that something horrible would happen to us. I took in his fear of *not having* and owned it as mine.

Dad grew up in the Depression and frequently went without. I began to formulate my self-worth as a young child based on his anger, fear, and self-doubt about his ability to be successful at work and to provide for the needs of ten children. He could not lovingly affirm me, therefore, I concluded, I was worth little.

It was terrifying to think of not working and bringing home a paycheck. With this decision, I'd be leaving the focus on my career; my dream of having a private psychotherapy practice was crushed after working so hard for this goal. Now, I would have to totally depend on others.

I considered how much I valued others. How much I gave to my teachers when I was in graduate school. How I gave one hundred percent of myself to my work and my clients. I set my resolve to give one hundred percent to myself for this time of healing.

But I could not help wondering, *Where was God taking me?*

Since being diagnosed, four different people suggested I contact a Chinese herbalist and healer (a tumor specialist from China) for information on using Chinese herbs along with chemotherapy. I had no idea of what the Chinese herbs might do for me. It was a leap of faith. At the time, praying for God's guidance became a constant mantra. Buzz, Laurie and I had quickly discovered the reams and reams of sometimes confusing information and suggestions for alternative treatments. Therefore, when four separate people asked if I had considered taking Chinese herbs along with chemotherapy, the idea held a lot of weight. All four recommended the same Chinese herbalist. It was too synchronistic to ignore.

His office was an hour away from my home in a small, two-story shopping mall that contained other shops that catered to oriental clientele. We passed a travel agency, clothing store and several Chinese restaurants that banked a common eating area on the way to the elevator. My hungry stomach immediately noticed that the air was saturated with the spices of oriental cooking. Riding up to the second floor it felt as if we were in another world.

His waiting room smelled different. It had a rather earthy scent that neither Buzz nor I could identify. We reasoned the smell came from the exotic Chinese herbs loaded on shelves near the front desk. Soon after we were seated my name was called and we were ushered into the doctor's office.

The office was sparsely furnished with several chairs in front of his large desk. It felt spacious and light with many windows along the top of one wall. I had never met a Chinese herbalist before, and found him to be a very pleasant man, with a rather small, thin build, slightly balding, glasses and crooked teeth. As we entered, he smiled, shook our hands and sat down. He read the intake information and with a mild Chinese accent, asked me to stick out my tongue. When I did, he shook his head a little, as if he saw what he expected to see. Then he took my wrist and carefully, with his eyes closed listened to my pulse moving his fingers in several different places. Finally, he looked at my short fingernails.

Silently, he began to write on a piece of paper, listing all the herbs that he wanted me to take. And then, signaling our appointment was over, he explained, "In Chinese medicine we can determine what is wrong by listening to the pulse. There are many, many different pulse readings that correspond to different illnesses. The color of the tongue, the shape and color of the fingernails and the size of the half-moons will also give clues as to what is wrong. We are very different from Western medicine!" Buzz and I looked at him and nodded in agreement. He then added, "Chinese medicine focuses on prevention, whereas Western medicine focuses more on diagnoses and treatment."

We were struggling with life and death decisions. What if I die because I didn't use an alternative treatment that had promise? Chinese herbs have been around for centuries. Toxic chemotherapy drugs balanced with the earth's natural herbs seemed right to Buzz and me.

But they are expensive. Five hundred dollars for one month. I was weak with shock. I gasped holding onto the counter and looked at Buzz. Buzz did not hesitate, quickly saying, "We will find a way," and handed over the charge card.

Whenever I look back at that experience I am filled with tears of gratitude for Buzz.

Following the herbalist's directions, every morning I boiled, strained, and drank the herbal cocktail (now available in pill form,), which tasted like stewed tree bark. I felt sorry for myself, couldn't these herbs at least taste decent since they cost so much!

Preparing the herbal cocktail every morning for four months was laborious, costly and tasted hideous. Did I remember to mention the cost and hideous taste? But I trusted the Chinese way to protect me from the toxicity of the chemotherapy, most especially, my heart. These herbs have been used successfully for many, many years in China.

I sensed my body would need their help. I was right. Each time I took them, I voiced a short prayer of thanks and asked them to protect me. After a while, they became a regular part of my healing regimen and I did not resent taking them. They became a sort of protective shield along with the chemotherapy drugs that would kill the cancer cells. Eventually, I saw them both as allies.

Later, we discovered the combo of Chinese herbs did help my heart from being devastated by chemotherapy. Chemotherapy drugs can be toxic to the heart. Standard procedure was to have a heart test prior to and after chemotherapy. The post chemotherapy heart test showed a slightly stronger heart function than before chemotherapy! I was struck with how important they were to my physical healing.

To this day, every day, I drink his recommended herbal teas, Reishi Tea for the immune system and Liver Peace, to cleanse the liver.

Soon after I attended another retreat at the Cenacle as a gift from my mother, I was able to make my treatment decision. Vivacious, full of life, and enthusiastic, Amy Harwell, the retreat presenter and author of *Ready to Live, Prepared to Die,* shared her cancer story. For the first time, I felt free to talk about the elephant in the room – the possibility of dying – *death.* Amy was told she had a very short time to live, so she made a list of BIDs (Before I Die), put her affairs in order, planned her funeral down to the last detail, and took off for the Galapagos Islands to swim with the sea lions.

Of course, she did not die.

Instead she discovered a precious truth: When you are prepared to die, spiritually, emotionally, down to the last funeral decision, you suddenly have all the energy you put toward the fear of dying into living. What freedom!

I made a decision to make peace with death, to investigate what I am so fearful of, to be prepared to die whenever that time comes.

I began my own list of BIDs:

- visit the American West
- go on vacation with my sisters
- visit my beloved Uncle Nard
- grow more vibrant perennials

In preparing for death, a recurring fear kept surfacing. *What if the energy I used to focus on dying made death happen?* As I grew closer to the heart of God, through prayer, spiritual reading and the loving concern of friends and family, my feelings of warmth, peace, and love were intense. Sometimes I would stop and remind God I want to live, that I am not ready to die. Amy reassured me these were normal emotions. The decision to face death was terrifying. Once I realized the connection between my underlying fear of death and how it was sapping my life energy, that same energy I needed to heal and stay healthy, the seed was planted. I had to make a treatment decision, so I decided to set this 'looking at death' aside, just long enough for me to focus on choosing an oncologist and a treatment protocol.

Several weeks later, on one of those unusually cool days in August, I was sitting on the front porch reading a scripture passage:

The Lord lives! Praise be to my Rock!
Exalted be God the Rock, My Savior! 2 Samuel 22:47

God will be my rock, strong, immovable, a constant, steady presence. Sitting on a table in front of me was a lovely stone given to me by a concerned friend. I held this beautiful white crystal rock in my hand, turning it over and over while admiring its many facets, reminding me of St. Teresa's many 'mansions' symbolizing the dwelling places of God. Holding the crystal over my heart I prayed to draw closer to the heart of God. When I was finished praying, I made a decision to trust Chaitan's first choice.

I chose Northwestern Medical Hospital. Bottom line, I felt comfortable in that waiting room on my first visit. Sure, it was small and crowded, but there was a beautiful vase of fresh flowers on a center table. Those flowers reminded me of the beauty that exists in our world. The other reasons:

- All the nurses and office staff were kind and helpful.
- My chosen oncologist was open to alternative therapies. He was also a compassionate doctor who believed in mystery and knew he didn't have all the answers.

My Treatment Protocol:

CHOP, which is a chemotherapy cocktail devised to eliminate any large-cell lymphoma and, monoclonal antibodies, (Rituxan, experimental, but promising) to treat the small-cell, indolent lymphoma.

I added a few holistic ingredients to this recipe:

- I was already taking Chinese herbs, and combined them with healthy nutrition for whole-body maintenance and support.
- Daily meditation along with guided imagery.
- Giving myself permission to focus on my needs.

- Gratefully accepting and asking for help when needed.

Since deciding on Northwestern and an actual treatment protocol, I kept reminding myself *this is really real.* Heaviness, fear and relief occupied my thoughts. Pulling together and organizing details at work gave me a focus. As I terminated my clients, I told each one I would be back in four months, knowing I had no idea where I would be in four months.

This was such a new concept of *focusing on me* – no outside work, concentrating on my interior rather than focusing on fixing for others. I needed to shift into the what-do-I-need mode of thinking. It was a question of life or death. For me taking care of myself was difficult. My self-worth depended on what I produced. I knew I needed to change. That was my work and no one could do it for me.

The children were older and more responsible, which I considered a blessing. Now that I'd made a final treatment decision, Buzz threw himself into his business to keep us financially stable. He gave me the gift of his blessing and support so I could focus on healing. I was grateful beyond words.

It was uncertain if I would be accepted for the Northwestern Monoclonal Antibody Rituxan Study. More tests needed to be completed. I was being inducted into the 'spiritual' experience of what it means to *wait.* My original concept was no longer valid. When you have a serious illness, waiting for test results, waiting for doctors, waiting to see if treatment has had the desired outcome take the word *wait* to a whole new level.

I awakened to knowing I have a choice. I could wait, constantly asking what if, *or* I could surrender to what is. I could come back to the present moment, breathe and *live.*

Easily said. How could I stay in the present? This was a monumental challenge for someone like me whose middle name is Fear and Trepidation.

Thich Nhat Hahn, a Buddhist monk and prolific writer, teaches if you live in the past with rumination and regret and focus on the future with fear and catastrophizing, you miss the present moment and consequently, miss life. I made a conscious decision to be in the present moment as a lifetime goal. In those moments when I was deeply aware of the *now*, it brought me joy, peace, and a rich sense of well-being.

September 1995

"Not until we are lost do we begin to understand ourselves."
~Henry David Thoreau

With chemotherapy looming, I focused on both nutrition to support my body, and those expensive Chinese herbs. Abby, and her husband, Jim, bought me a Champion Juicer, the 'king' of all juicers. A licensed clinical nutritionist prescribed juicing to counter my years of eating too many carbs – substituting popcorn for dinner and candy bars for lunch in the interest of time. After reading the instructions for this large impressive machine, and assembling the parts, I washed and peeled what I thought might be enough raw carrots for a glass of juice. Each carrot needed to be fed into the jaws of the grinder. I was mesmerized by the power of this machine to produce liquid from this rather hard vegetable and proud of myself for the effort. Drinking my first glass of fresh carrot juice tasted strange, however, the idea of drinking the essence of six carrots felt healthy. Juicing fresh vegetables daily became a part of my new, nutritious diet.

It was now time to shop for a wig. Laurie and I spent a day looking for one that felt comfortable and looked stylish. The samples looked horrible, but I finally found one that looked reasonably real. A friend who had chemotherapy shared with me that all her hair fell out—eyelashes, eyebrows, everything. In some ways, anticipating the loss of my hair seemed to be the most difficult part of accepting the cancer diagnosis. Such a shallow thought, I know. There are so many other parts of this life threating illness that are far more terrifying. A dear friend, Marianne, did not think that was so surprising, as she reminded me, "You are a Libra, ruled by Venus, the goddess of love and beauty." Depressed and on the verge of tears many times that day, hibernation seemed like a great idea. At the same time, I was trying to catch myself and not project into future what-ifs. Who knew what would fall out?

After the wig shopping, I came home to receive a message from Northwestern Hospital. My heart sunk as I listened. They required another blood sample before they would make a decision as to whether I could be a part of the experimental protocol. I inwardly groaned, "Oh, God one more test. What if I did not qualify for the protocol? Would my life depend on this one final blood test?"

While waiting for the test results, I attended a baby shower with a friend. Happy to see her, I was surprised at my discomfort being with her as the day progressed. There was an aura of judgment that surrounded her. If anyone did not meet her criteria for biblical correctness, they were deemed to be in 'spiritual error' and would be led astray by authors who are not biblically based. Many Christians fear the New Age movement and seem to be terrified of any concept that does not come directly from Scripture. To them the only truth (literally translated) comes from the biblical context of first and second century writings.

Will not the request of any soul, regardless of faith tradition, seeking a spiritual connection with God, a connection not based on ego, be blessed and honored? God will lead us where we need to go. Who is to judge what gift will or won't come from New Age insights? Growing up in a fear-based denomination, I have seen myself blossom into acceptance, recognition, and gratitude for the gift in all spiritualties. How can I 'love my neighbor' if I feel I have the only truth and way to the Source? Is God's love exclusive to one way of thinking and believing? Is Gandhi in hell because he did not 'confess with his lips that Jesus is Lord?' I was becoming uncomfortable with rigid, judgmental, black and white dualistic thinking. In the not so recent past, it was difficult for me to access the Sacred because I thought I already knew the truth – that being what I already agreed with and what did not frighten or threaten me. With this attitude, my spiritual intake valve was small, tight and guarded. I was not completely open to this mysterious, infinitely loving, unknowable God.

I once heard a story about God's love. A woman had a son who went to prison for terrible crimes. The mother died of her grief. Soon after, her son also died and stood before the throne of God. In seeing her prodigal son, his mother, who was standing close to God's throne, walked down from the throne and wrapped her arms around her child in a loving embrace. Surely, God loves us at least as much as a mother loves her child.

Devastated and frightened by the cancer diagnosis, my eighty-one-year-old mother felt helpless. A consummate prayer warrior, she commandeered *everyone* (mailman, sales clerks, and whomever she came in contact with) to pray with her for her daughter. I was grateful, and yet, angry and impatient with her. When she called, she talked at great length, wouldn't ask if it was a good time, or even ask how I was doing. When we were together, she would end our visit with a hug and a deep sigh, while for a moment, hanging on to me.

As the oldest and only daughter growing up in the depression with six younger brothers, my mother, Corinne, was treated as if she were an only child. She had her own room and all her own clothes. Several of her brothers' thought she was selfish, insensitive, and that the world revolved around her needs and wants. Petite with a shapely figure, thick brown hair peppered with auburn highlights, brown eyes and an infectious laugh, Mom was very attractive. She was smart in school, musically talented, and always told me, "Mama did not ask anything of me except, I must complete my school work and practice the piano."

There was a narcissistic trait in Mom honed by her parents. She really did not know how to help me. This was a Mother who never offered to help with the dishes if she were invited over for dinner, or offered to prepare a meal if I were ill. I hesitated to share my concerns with her, for fear of how she might react. I did not have the energy to buoy her up. Remembering past behaviors, I witnessed growing up, I wondered, would she cry? Go into a depression? Create a scene? Become angry? Well, I was no longer a child and resolved to face this issue.

One afternoon, while sitting at her round, blue tile kitchen table sharing a pot of tea, we began the conversation with chitchat about my children. We quickly moved into when I would start chemotherapy. Taking a deep breath and in the most sensitive way I could manage, I said, "Mom, I know this is not easy for you, but there are many unknowns that come with a cancer diagnosis. I want to tell you what I need from you so you can help me." Waiting to see her reaction, I paused. With her elbow on the table, she casually rested her chin on her hand and waited expectantly.

"When you call me," I continued, "you often don't ask me if this is a good time. When you hug me you hang onto me, as if you expect me to buoy you up with hugs and encouragement. I do not have the energy now. I need you to support me to the best of your ability."

Mom's eyes widened as I spoke. Her full attention was on what I was saying. Occasionally, she put her hand over her heart and would lean toward me. In a very grave, gracious and understanding manner, she asked, "How can I better help you?" Then she added, "Be specific. I want to know how I am hugging you that feels as if I am hanging on you," and then she wanted me to show her so she could get it right. Relieved and grateful, I realized our relationship had moved to a deeper level.

I was no longer a little girl without a voice.

I was often struck by the seriousness of the disease. The outcome would be terminal if I chose no treatment and, it could be terminal even if I followed through with a treatment. Sometimes when I saw people, I wondered if they were aware of what it's like to be in such a life-and-death struggle. It was difficult to stay in places long. 'Chitchat' was no longer fun. Sad, scared and displaced, I did dishes and folded clothes, thinking of these ordinary activities done so many times. I think *I will be safe here doing dishes, or folding clothes in the basement. No cancer can get me here.*

Later, Buzz shared he was consumed with the thought of losing me, his wife, the mother of his children, and the possibility of financial ruin and that his life was spiraling out of control. However, he told me, there was also a sense of pride in his sobriety and health and a feeling of … 'I can do this!' He showed up for our family and me with his heart and eyes wide open. He held the ground for all of us while I sorted out how I needed to take care of myself.

I had purchased a wig, implemented a healthy nutritional regimen, ordered guided imagery tapes, chose an oncologist and a treatment protocol. I was ready. All I needed was acceptance into the experimental study.

Chapter 5 – Treatment Begins

"The death of fear is doing what you fear to do."
~Sequichie Comingdeer

Early one Monday morning, my youngest daughter Mindy, who was ten at the time, shook my shoulder to wake me up. "Mom, Northwestern Hospital is on the phone. They want to speak to you!" I quickly sat up and shook my head trying to wake up – to clear my head and sound coherent. *This is it!* I thought, *the blood test results are back!* With my heart pounding, I croaked with my just-waking-up-voice,
"Hello?"
A feminine voice responded, "Hello, is this Deborah Marqui?"
I replied, my voice faint. "Yes."
"This is Anna, the doctor's research assistant. I am pleased to tell you that you have been accepted into the monoclonal experimental protocol."
I could barely focus on her next instructions. I was giddy with relief.
She continued. "Your treatment will be administered in alternating phases. First, you will receive the experimental drug, Rituxan, and then one-week later chemotherapy. You will receive a total of six rounds of chemotherapy. Can you be at the hospital two weeks from today to begin treatment?"
"Absolutely, I will be there."
On the appointed day of treatment with the new drug, Laurie drove me to the hospital. She dropped me off at the hospital front entrance and then parked the car in the massive, multi-layered parking garage. Each floor was named after a famous singer to help folks remember where to locate their cars, and to jog the memory even more, the song that made

these singers famous played continuously on each floor. I would like to thank the mastermind who thought of the idea. Hearing a grim medical diagnosis or worried about a loved one, a person can barely remember their name, let alone find a parked car in that vast, layered sea of vehicles.

I waited for Laurie in the lobby and we walked to the Hematology Oncology Department. I was soon taken to a small room with a bed and several machines that would monitor the drug injection. By this time, I did not care about hospital policy, I wanted Laurie with me at all times. I felt safer. And she did, too. With her methodical, technical mind, she missed very little – always asking questions desiring to understand what the doctors and nurses were doing and why. Sometimes I could sense an edge of irritation to their voices as the medical personnel replied to Laurie's many queries. *That's just too bad. Relax and answer her questions,* I told myself. *She will not let go until she understands what you are doing.*

I came armed with my readings, a cassette player to help me with guided imagery, and my journal. They wheeled in some equipment to test my heart function. It was protocol to test before and after the chemo regimen to be sure my heart could handle treatment. Then, sitting on the edge of the bed, with my journal, readings and tape player nearby, the nurse injected a large dose of Benadryl to offset any allergic reaction to the Rituxan. I immediately fell back onto the bed and went to sleep – and slept all the way through treatment and all the way home. No reading, no tape listening, no journaling.

The next day began slowly, but I gradually felt more energized. I did not feel tired at all – a pleasant change. Buzz and I had a 'nooner' that day, which was loving and tender, probably the source of this extra energy boost! I did laundry and cleaned – ordinary tasks helped me feel normal and safe. I really hoped the chemo would have the same effect on me. My sons, Matt and Nick, periodically stopped in to see how I was doing. I might have been sitting at the counter in the kitchen when they came in and they each would gently put their hands on my shoulder and ask, "How are you doing, Mom?"

In their sweet asking I could see the fear and concern in their eyes, masked by their stoicism. I am also trying to be stoic and brave in front of my children. "I'm OK," I say. The truth was I didn't know how to respond to my children in the emotional state I found myself in. Sometimes I was okay, but often I was an emotional mess. How could I know what to share, if I didn't even know myself on that hellish roller coaster ride?

I think we all cried alone. It made me sad we couldn't cry together.

I was struck by how much I loved my sons – thoughtful, loyal, kind, sense of humor, industrious – they are good men. Pride filled my heart whenever I thought of the men they had become.

As I was waiting to begin the first round of chemotherapy, I experienced another dream:

Mindy brings home small animals that we keep in a glass container filled with grass. We thought they might be reproducing, so we decided to burn the grass so we could see what is happening. The grass burned quickly. I thought all the animals were killed; however, several mice and one small cow remained. They looked strong and unaffected by the fire. We were surprised.

The unconscious often uses symbols from daily life for dream material. The previous day, Mindy, in her love for animals, brought home some baby mice she found outside and was feeding them milk with an eyedropper.

The dream was a symbol of the cleansing I would have to go through with the fire of chemotherapy. Like the mice and cow, I would come out unharmed and strong – in body and soul. Cows are by nature docile and passive, animals that obey without question. I am certainly a person who follows the rules – which feels safe to  me. However, I need to 'step out of the box' and decide what is right for me – whether it is mainstream treatment or not. Monoclonal antibodies (Rituxan) have a mouse protein molecule attached to the antibody. The dream was a confirmation of the treatment protocol I had chosen.

The day before my first chemotherapy treatment, a port-a-cath was inserted surgically under my skin below the collarbone. This would allow the chemotherapy to be injected into my body without damaging the veins in my arm. It was painful and uncomfortable. It was Laurie's idea that we stay in the city at a hotel near the hospital. What a wonderful idea! We read magazines, leisurely talked, watched movies, laughed and even shopped before the port-a-cath procedure. What a great way to spend these last three days. It made the waiting bearable.

I wanted to feel positive toward this chemo-cocktail called CHOP:

C for Cytoxan
H for Doxorubicin
O for Vincristine
P for Prednisone

All of these medicines have very scary possible side effects. They even sound scary and formidable. On the day I was accepted into the treatment protocol I was given a sheet to sign that listed all of the possible side effects from these chemo drugs. The list was over a page long! I opted not to read it, fearful I would focus on what 'might' happen and concerned my body would respond to these negative thoughts. Besides I knew I needed the 'big guns' for this disease. I wondered would the baby get thrown out with the bath water? The day of my first chemotherapy finally arrived. Seated in a small, crowded and very silent waiting room, I was wedged between Laurie on my right and a middle-aged man on my left wearing a baseball cap and a Chicago Bulls t-shirt. Is he an advocate or a patient I wondered? Looking around the room, I see quiet tenseness, eyes lowered, covered baldheads, pale, hairless complexions, some people in wheel chairs. My eyes welled with tears as I listened to my guided imagery tapes. Aware that my heart was beating wildly, I whispered to myself, "Stay positive."

Seeing my headphones and assuming I am listening to the radio, the man on my left tapped my shoulder and asked, "Do you have the Bulls score?"

I burst out laughing at this perfectly sane question for all of us living in or around Chicago. In this insane place, where my life is hanging in the balance, someone wants to know the score of a basketball game! The healing power of humor helped me face this first 'prairie burn.'

When it was my turn, the oncology nurse, took Laurie and me into a small room and motioned for me to sit in a large 'Barkalounger.' There was a drip bag next to the chair. She patiently explained the process that could take about an hour:

- Ativan to calm me down
- Zofran to counter nausea
- Compazine to help with nausea and anxiety

She repeated the same information the oncologist gave me. "Often after the first week of receiving the chemo drugs, you might experience some strong reactions of fatigue and low white blood counts. Your body is fighting the toxins that are killing the cancer cells. Around the second or third week you should feel better, but everyone is different." Then she administered the CHOP through the porta-cath. I held my breath waiting to feel something as the toxic medicine coursed through my veins, but nothing happened. I listened to my positive tapes while Laurie read.

The next day I was mentally positive. I wondered if it was the anti-anxiety meds? I had no nausea, only a slightly upset stomach, fatigue, a drippy sinus, and a dry mouth with a metallic taste and a burning, tingling sensation. Every morning, as I applied moisturizing cream to my face, I ran my fingers over the enlarged lymph node on my neck. The node had already gotten smaller! I was surprised at the speed. The nurses said that sometimes happens. Gratitude filled my heart that the chemotherapy was actually working.

I wanted to attend a retreat at the Cenacle on integrating body, mind, and spirit the first weekend after chemotherapy. It seemed a good idea. However, when I arrived, strange uncomfortable sensations announced their presence in my bladder. I had not had a bowel movement that day, which was very unusual for me. The toxic side effects of chemotherapy began that weekend and quickly gained momentum. Unaware of what to expect, I decided to stay at the retreat. I wrote in my journal:

The retreat has begun. We are to address several questions: Where am I in my body experience? Where am I in relation to my body? I reflect: Since starting treatment I feel a tentative relationship with my body. A relationship that is guarded and wary, watching for side effects of the chemo and trying to circumvent any problems by nutrition, visualization, and rest.

Accustomed to excellent health, this experience is foreign. I am passing through a fire of purification. I will make it through as a 'super star,' not as a martyr. This awareness brings me great comfort and purpose.

There is a strange excitement as I face the unknown and grow from this experience. What will I learn? All of the exterior stimuli of my life have increased tenfold as I take in and recognize the ineffable beauty of Buzz, my children, Nature, friends, books, prayer, food – everything. I realize I must take time in order for my body to heal. If not now, when? My life depends on it.

The presenter rambled on and I could hardly stand it, yet she had an honest, earthy quality that I liked. We are to consider and journal about another question: What experiences have you had with your body?

I remember:

- *Holding hands and walking downtown with Dad when I was five years old*
- *My first kiss as a sophomore in high school from Jack C. who was killed in Vietnam*
- *Jumping rope as a child*

81

- *Euphoric feeling after the birth of Matt, my first child*
- *First orgasm*
- *Learning to tango with Buzz*

Next question:

What is my body saying to me in this quiet place? I write:

Nothing. I am sick of writing. Others are fidgeting, too.

The presenter says, "Five more minutes."

Inwardly I groan. *I feel defiant. I realize it is not the material being presented. I have no business being somewhere other than home three days after receiving chemotherapy. One more day, should I go home?* I stay and continue to journal:

That evening at the retreat, I started to read <u>Sleeping with Bread</u> by Matt, Dennis, and Sheila Linn. The authors suggest asking yourself terrific, healing questions each night before you go to bed, a process to help examine your day from the writings of St. Ignatius of Loyola, so I ask myself:

What was I grateful for today?
What was I not so grateful for?
When did I feel most alive?
When did I feel life draining out of me?

Yesterday, I felt most alive when sharing or connecting with another person. I felt most drained when my focus was lost and I wondered if I was learning anything and going into the cancer world of 'what if?' Today I felt most alive being the center of attention at the dinner table when talking about cancer and my first orgasm!

The authors say that when you do this exercise every day you will gain a solid understanding of what brings you consolation and what brings you desolation. Once you figure out what brings you consolation, do more of it. The Linn's also discussed how this exercise helps to guide you when you are making decisions. I was happy to be going home.

Six days after CHOP, my body responded to this toxic cocktail. My throat was covered with sores from a yeast infection, taking me back to the days as a child when I was often sick with tonsillitis. I ached everywhere; sometimes feeling like daggers had been inserted into my abdomen. I could see why people starve to death on these drugs; everything tasted like metal. I took my Chinese herbs, wondering if they were helping, catching myself doubting the power they were supposed to be wielding.

Chapter 6 – The Prairie Burn of Chemotherapy

"I prayed like a man walking in a forest at night, feeling his way with his hands, at each step fearing to fall into pure bottomlessness forever. Prayer is like lying awake at night, afraid, with your head under the cover, hearing only the beating of your own heart.

~Wendell Berry

October 1995

Too sick to write in my journal, I spoke instead. A deep part of me needed to give voice to this journey. Speaking into a recorder was wearisome but writing was impossible. And so, I spoke in whispers into a small cassette player that I kept at my bedside. In the middle of the night I would waken, curled up in a ball lying on my side and reach for the recorder. I felt like Job, tested beyond anything I could have imagined, physically consumed by the toxic, yet necessary 'prairie burn' of chemotherapy. These are my word for word transcribed recordings with a few changes to make them more coherent.

Chemotherapy

This chemotherapy experience is incredibly painful, physically painful. First to appear were mouth sores that felt like a horrific case of strep throat, which lasted for two to three days until I was given medication. Constipation was next. Never having experienced problems with my bowel, going one week without a bowel movement was excruciating. I felt like I was ninety years old, weak, with aches and pains everywhere. My white blood count tested 1000 (normal is about 10,000). The doctor told me, "You must be very careful now, try not to be exposed to germs, as your immune system will not be able to fight back." Everything is a struggle.

Homecoming

Tonight is Alyce's Junior/Senior Homecoming Dance. She is my sixteen-year-old daughter and third child. She is bursting with excitement and looks absolutely radiant. Her date is Carl, a sweet, young man who still had the price tags from his new sport coat dangling from his sleeve, which the mother in me immediately came out and I helped him remove them. In the back of my mind, I wondered if that was all I had left. That the mother instinct was going to be the last to go.

I was sad his parents didn't come. I am supposed to wear a mask around people, but I could not bring myself to put it on, as it was hot and uncomfortable. I stepped back from everyone. I enjoyed just seeing people, but I was afraid to be in the same room.

This is really tough.

Decisions

My women's prayer group meets tomorrow. I am looking forward to it, but afraid to be around people. On a regimen of stool softeners, going from feeling constipated to having diarrhea, I'm afraid to leave the house. This disease is literally a crapshoot. I am inundated with information about what to do from the straight Western medical world and from the alternative medicine world. What to do about the effects of chemotherapy on my body is my decision and, once again, I need to move forward and make a decision. What additional therapies can I take that will help my body tolerate the toxic chemotherapy and yet allow the chemotherapy to do its work? I'm still taking the Chinese herbs and wondering if they are helping at all. If they are, I can't imagine how much rougher this process would be without them, and don't want to find out.

I wonder if my body will ever be normal again.

Disappointment

Another restless night, with a strange pain in my stomach and bowels. Something isn't right. It's a beautiful fall day with the sun shining and I think things will get better. I will feel better. Concerned about my body and scared about facing the next round of chemotherapy, I keep wondering what will happen to me. I try to be positive and listen to meditation tapes. I need to listen to the tapes more often.

Yesterday, Buzz told me that a client he was doing a huge addition for called and told him that they signed with another contractor. They felt fearful that his loyalty would be to me first and they had too much riding on the addition. Buzz was disappointed and rightly so. I felt responsible, angry, and discriminated against. Buzz was sweet and said things happen for a reason and perhaps this was for the best. We need the money. I feel terrible.

Kindness

My nephew, John, and his sweet wife came by yesterday. She is about three months pregnant and showed me her little tummy. They seem so focused and goal-oriented.

I found myself feeling sad that Buzz and I weren't more like them in our young, married life. From their precious, hard-earned money they gave me a gift certificate. I was moved. This morning, I feel ashamed to be taking their money. She could be buying a cute maternity outfit.

Being on the receiving end and knowing I need help is humbling, especially because I pride myself on self-sufficiency, a deeply entrenched Western world belief. *Pull yourself up by the bootstraps – I don't need your help – I can do it myself – I don't want to bother you –* all these messages ring in my ears. The truth is, everyone has a need to give, a need to share the love and caring we all hold in our hearts. There is a knowing in our DNA that love is the most powerful force in the universe. It is love that heals.

As the one who is now in need of others' caring, I must let go, and, with gratitude, become the opportunity for others to fulfill that need to give.

Fighting

I feel frustrated. The teaching hospital is an hour away. I don't feel cared for. It's difficult to reach the oncology nurses. There was a mix-up with the instructions on how to relieve the constipation, no initial instructions on what to do if I developed a yeast infection in my mouth. I think their staff is stretched with many stressed and frightened patients. There is so much pressure and I don't think they turn too many patients away. I would not have wanted them to turn me away. They are stretched thin.

I am also recognizing a tendency in me to not want to bother anyone. Bernie Siegel says you have to fight for yourself, make those calls, and be a bother. He is right. It is my *life*.

Friendship

One-day last week, I called a dear friend, Dawn, crying. I was in pain and scared. "I'm coming over," she said, and she did. She even crawled into bed with me and we hugged and cried. Then, she drew a hot bath for me. While I soaked, she did my dishes.

Afterward, we had tea and talked about our children, about what is happening in our lives, about what God is teaching me in this cancer journey. Currently, the lesson seems to be that I need to be vigilant in expressing my feelings, owning them, feeling them, and giving them back to God. It is only then that emotional healing will follow. My feelings are a part of me and I can't keep tucking them away. Like the other day, when my nephew gave me the gift certificate and I felt ashamed and didn't want to think about it. I need to think about it and I need to feel it. That is one of the major lessons God is teaching me today. Maybe in learning how to do this, I will begin to love myself, and, in the process strengthen my entire body. It's a message sent to my immune system: everything about me is okay. I find myself okay, I love myself enough to take the time to do what I need to heal body, mind, and spirit. I will become more mindful of my days, what happened and how I felt. I will own my feelings and express them in appropriate ways.

I thanked Dawn for her thoughtfulness. And, I have to say, that was the most wonderful gift and it was just what I needed. She came back the next day with her sweet, young daughters and cleaned my house.

Mindfulness

Being mindful of each day makes sense to me. It's so beautiful, so simple, so healthy. I will do it now. What brought me the most consolation several days ago was preparing the house for Alyce and the Homecoming picture taking. I didn't do heavy cleaning, just simple things, like fiddling with a picture, changing a picture, making a flower arrangement.

90

Being creative brought me consolation. In those moments when using my artistic imagination, I was no longer in earth-time but, as the Greek's would say, 'Kairos' time or God's time.

What was I least grateful for that day? Quickly, I remembered after taking medicine for the constipation, instead of being impacted up to my eyeballs I was going to the bathroom every five minutes. While folding clothes in the basement I could not make it upstairs to the bathroom quickly enough and pooped in my pants. No matter how hard I tried to hold it in, it just kept coming. I felt helpless, embarrassed, and out of control. This incident seemed like a metaphor for my life right now.

The question I kept asking myself over and over was – Can *I allow myself to feel helpless and out of control*?

PLOM (Poor little ol' me)

I was thrilled to have a normal bowel movement today. It's amazing how such a small thing could bring exuberant joy and relief! I don't think I will ever take a normal bowel movement for granted again.

I'm still having terrible pains in my abdomen and I don't know why. Uncertain and scared, I'm waiting for a call back from the nurse. I experienced a difficult night. If I don't hear back, will I need to go through another night of pain? I'm feeling like PLOM (poor little ol' me). Everyone is gone, doing 'normal' activities. It's quiet at home and I feel abandoned. My sister Ann is visiting and is out shopping with my other sisters and sister-in-law. It's a beautiful fall day. I want to be with them, but too uncomfortable to go. Maybe I'll get up and get dressed. I don't feel like it, but I think I will. I'll try to call the hospital again.

Maybe I should see a lower GI doctor.

Women's Group

My women's prayer group met yesterday at my sister's. We started by singing some beautiful songs that moved my heart, then the conversation quickly turned into a heated discussion about the pope and politics. There was no candle lit, no opening prayer. I began to feel irritated and frustrated. The meeting wasn't going the way *I* wanted. I had invited my close evangelical friend and fretted about what she must be thinking when the conversation turned to denominational crap. Finally, the girls began to talk about what God was doing in their lives, which is what I wanted to hear. I wanted the women to share their faith walk and how God is present to them and what God is currently teaching them. This kind of sharing is where I draw strength.

Politics are important to my sister, so I try to be patient. I notice lately my patience levels are becoming thinner. It is difficult for me to sit still. I am anxious to get to the meat of what I feel is important. With a life-threatening illness, I have little interest in the 'chaff of life.' I only want the wheat. We prayed for a friend who has breast cancer and then for me, which was powerful and comforting.

Meltdown

Yesterday I experienced a meltdown. As I am physically sinking lower and lower, with a rising fever and pain in my abdomen and lower back, my family goes about their normal lives, ignoring me.

How could you be so selfish? I screamed at my girls and husband. Call someone. I need help!

I was angry at Buzz for not being more of an advocate for me. I thought he would be more aggressive about helping me get to the bottom of this intense pain, getting on the phone and demanding some help and answers. He said he feels damned if he does and damned if he doesn't, that he can't do anything right.

I was finally admitted to a local hospital last night. Due to a mix-up, I could not reach my oncologist who was out of town or his alternate. Buzz called an oncologist who was connected to a nearby hospital. Because my white blood count is so low, I have an infection, but they don't know where. I am in a private room. Everyone has to wear a mask.

Last night as they wheeled me down a hospital corridor to my room, I counted acoustical tiles thinking: This is not me. I'm not here. This simply cannot be that I have joined the ranks of the seriously ill.

Hospital

Day One – Fever

I am in the hospital with a fever hooked up to antibiotics. This is scary. They can't find the source of the infection, which, the doctor says, is common when white blood cell counts are so low. As the fever starts to spike, I take Tylenol and sweat bullets waiting for the fever to go down. Then, it slowly rises, and I huddle under the blankets, freezing. I go through the whole process again and again. I'm really afraid.

Many people have called or visited. I feel overwhelmed with the outpouring of love and concern. My younger sister, Corinne, called last night and something she said helped me realize how frightened everyone is. I can't remember what she said; perhaps it was the concern in her voice.

Buzz is frightened, too. So afraid his wife might die. He said he feels like an 'emotional zombie.' Insurance would not cover shots to bring my white count up, $1,000.00 each – he said, "Bring them on!" To him it seems like 'good-bye,' wrapped in an extended nightmare of confusion, helplessness and frightened to the core. "I see myself shifting toward accepting all that death presents to me – a dead wife, three dependent children, severe debt, and running a business and a household as an emotional wreck." I asked how he is able to cope – his answer was simple, "It is the assistance of friends and family that give their time, compassionate listening, financial help, and meals that sustains me." He added, "Previous petty judgments of these friends and family have melted away."

Day Two – Real

One afternoon, after school, Alyce came to visit me. She sat down on a chair next to the bed, wearing a protective mask. She looked intently at me and tears began to roll down her cheeks.

"This is real," she said, while quietly sobbing. "I just didn't realize how serious this is."

My heart breaks to see her frightened. I felt helpless and just as terrified.

Day Three – Dancing

My dear friend, Cathy, visited. She brought me a live recording of harp music called *Rapture* by Marjorie Valeri. Before she recorded the music, Marjorie had said:

I've been molding and nurturing this music inside of me for five years. It is the beauty of the soul. The spirit expressed though the human heart. I wanted to channel the exquisiteness of our being human with all its depths and heights, creating resonance between the two to create beauty. I'm very grateful for being a human being and I'm very grateful I can share this music with you.

The music was captivating. I closed my eyes and immediately found myself as an adult, dancing before Jesus, who responded with loving appreciation. He then held out his hands and danced with me. Later that evening, in a phone conversation, I shared this experience with Mindy. She asked me a wonderful question that caused me to reflect.

"But, Mom, what did He *say* to you?"

Pausing for a moment, my whole being filled with warmth as I reflected on the experience.

"Not a word was said between us. I expressed my love for him, my love of being, my love for my body and soul, and he just loved me back. Words were not needed." This experience reminded me of the words of Hafiz, the wise, Persian sage, *O listen – listen more carefully to what is inside you right now. In my world all that remains is the wondrous call to dance and prayer, rising up like a thousand suns out of the mouth of a single bird.*

Day Four – Surprised

My younger brother, John, came to visit. We are just two years apart. As children, we typically, argued, fought and played together. Often, my two older sisters and I thought he was too young to be included in on the important 'grown up' activities, like helping my parents put out the toys from Santa or staying out later with friends. But we were close enough in age to have fun pretending we were 'Big Men' who camped out or built houses. John loved to tease and hated to lose an argument.

He shyly and a little sheepishly came into the room and sat down. "Hi Debbie, how are you?"

It was the first time he talked with me since I was diagnosed in June and this was now October. "John, I feel really hurt after all these weeks you haven't called me."

Sitting in the chair across from the bed, guiltily, he said, "I have had a hard time dealing with this cancer diagnosis. I am really scared for you, so I just shelved it and tried not to think about it."

Then we had a healing conversation. We talked about how much courage it takes to confront the scary parts of ourselves and when an Albright (my maiden name) is angry, the first question he or she could ask is "What am I afraid of?" Fear seems to be the root of our anger and angst. We reminisced about our parents, who were completely opposite from each other in how they viewed life. Mom was the optimist, who saw the glass as half-full and all will be well. Emphatically, my Father, the pessimist, would say to her, "Corinne, you do not live in reality!"

Mom would say defiantly, "I don't want to live in *your* reality!"

As children, John and I agreed that we absorbed more of Dad's fear of life than Mom's optimistic attitude. Before John left, he prayed a beautiful healing prayer for me and then I prayed that God would heal the little boy in him that was frightened to face the scary parts of life. His visit was the highlight of my week.

Day Five – Gifts

Father Dempsey, my parish priest, visited. It was such a joy to talk with him, as he is one of the truly blessed and anointed priests who stress the infinite love of God. He told me he had his first and second graders praying for me. We spoke of the power in the prayers of the children. Then, he prayed with me.

Day Six – Siblings

Both Ann and Laurie came next, with my brother, Ted, who gave me a soft, pale blue, flowered cotton nightgown that still had the price tag of $85 attached in case I wanted to return it. My first thought was I am not worth an $85 nightgown. I will return it and buy several cheaper ones. I discarded that thought and gratefully accepted his gift. After they left, I put it on and savored the soft, rich material against my skin. I decided this nightgown was well worth the money. I was worth the money.

Day Seven – Mom

Mom came today and we had a nice visit. She asked me to tell her when I was feeling tired. So, I did. I was grateful she remembered our conversation weeks ago about my need for her to be sensitive to what I needed, instead of her sadness and fear dealing with one of her children being ill.

Matt and Nick both stopped by with Andy, their childhood friend. I was happy to see them. Felicity, another younger sister from Pennsylvania phoned that night, then my brother-in-law, Jack and my sister Corinne called. I was touched by everyone's loving concern.

Home

After a week in the hospital, I am finally home. What a relief not to have a fever. I felt very loved this week. I am happy to be home and happy to feel good. Oh, what a gift! I feel hopeful.

My hair is falling out in handfuls. What a shock. I washed my hair this morning and there was an enormous glob clogging the drain. When I combed my hair, clumps fell out. There are thin spots on the side of my head and crown. At this rate, in two days I will have no hair at all. Sometimes I think, *what the hell? Shave it all off.* It falls in my food; it's all over my pillow and the furniture. What an annoyance! I cannot picture myself bald, though. This is hard. My pubic hair is even falling out—how strange. If I consider the up side, I won't have to shave my legs and armpits for a while—that's a perk. I pray that my hair will grow back curly and thick, with blonde highlights and no gray.

Actually, I will take hair any way it comes.

Love and Laughter

People send their love: cards, gifts, flowers, phone calls, and meals – those treasured meals, organized by Dawn, that gave me inestimable comfort just knowing my family will have nutritious meals daily. I feel blessed and loved. It's unbelievable. I don't think I could say now that I wish I never had cancer. I would not have experienced this outpouring of love, or known or even believed it. What I find happening in my soul is that I am beginning to love me – and that is something new, exciting, and strange.

When I came home from the hospital, I putzed around the house until I felt tired and went to sleep. I dreamed I was laughing at myself over something, I can't remember what, but I woke up laughing. What pure joy to laugh! The dream was telling me that a sense of humor is an important part of healing.

Forgiveness

Several days after returning home from the hospital, I listened again to the tape of Valeri's harp music. The melody made me think about my childhood and children. Babies are loved and joyful. As they grow up, sometimes they are lied to about who they are. I considered how belief patterns begin to form in young psyches. Children think they are not lovable because they spilled their milk, or because they messed in their pants. Parents yell at them, friends call them names, or teachers humiliate them. Many children's belief systems are based on the anger that is hurdled at them. The lie that they are not worthy of love, nor are they as perfect as God made them is embedded in them.

I reflected on the earliest times I could remember when people had hurt me. Immediately, my kindergarten art teacher came to mind. Miss Taylor was an overweight, gray-haired, stern, mustached, unhappy woman. Not long after school began that fall, my kindergarten teacher instructed us to sit in a large circle. She told us that Miss Taylor, the art teacher, would come to give us an art lesson. Everyone was excited. Soon, Miss Taylor, in a huge art smock and squeaky earth shoes marched heavily into the room and barked out her wishes.

"Listen up kids! I want you to draw a picture of your house and family. I don't want to hear any conversation! Now get to work you have twenty minutes." I did not know how to draw people or a house, so I divided the paper into pie-shaped sections and colored each section a different color, very careful to stay in the lines. I thought it was quite beautiful. When we were finished, she instructed us to once again sit in a large circle. Miss Taylor then held up each picture in front of the class and commented on each one. Then she came to mine.

"What's *this?* I *told* you to draw a picture of your house and family!" Then, with a toss of her wrist, she threw it aside.

For the first time in my young life, I felt shame wash over me.

In everyone's life there are traumas. Big "T" traumas, such as incest, violence, sudden death, rape, war, and so many others, and little "t" traumas, such as being shamed by teachers, parents, bullied and excluded by your peers, parents withholding physical and emotional affection, and many others. Both kinds of trauma have the power to firmly entrench beliefs and messages about yourself that are not true. Replaying the hurt and imagining someone in the situation who loves you and is bigger and stronger than you were at the time of the trauma can be powerfully healing.

I clearly remembered that incident, in great detail, but this time I pictured Jesus taking me by the hand, as a five-year-old, and holding me in his lap, telling me how pretty the picture was, how perfect the lines were drawn, what beautiful colors I had chosen, and how neatly I had colored each section. Then, I tried to forgive Miss Taylor. Teachers have so much power!

Another school memory came to me. I am in fifth grade and wore a sundress without a slip. Looking through the armholes, anyone could see my flat chest. After recess, at the drinking fountain, Jim N. cruelly said, "There's Albright. A carpenter's dream: flat as a board." At first, I didn't understand what he was talking about and then it occurred to me what he meant. I was ashamed and embarrassed.

This was not an easy exercise, but there is a *knowing* that tells me forgiveness is at the heart of healing. And so, I created a list of people I wanted to forgive and began the process of forgiving, one by one.

Weak

Today, I feel physically weak. I don't ache or hurt, which is a relief and a blessing, I just feel very weak. It is difficult to walk. I have been forcing myself to walk around to regain strength. I juiced fresh carrots, spinach, and celery and felt good drinking it. I drank my Chinese herbs and then I looked at the empty glass. Are they hurting me or helping me, I wondered? I was afraid to stop for fear I would find they were all that was keeping me alive.

I have lost most of my hair. There are big bald spots and thin places on top of my head and around my ears. Picturing myself without hair is traumatic. I feel ugly, which taints my mood. At times, I lash out at my family, which produces guilt and remorse in me. I believe they look at me and think, "Oh, go back to the hospital. Things were much more peaceful without you!"

I'm still torn about shaving my head. My scalp tingles or hurts when I lie down. If I press hard into the pillow, sections of hair fall out, which is a strange prickly feeling. I tried on my wig yesterday. It looks better than I thought, however, it feels foreign, heavy, and tight, like a thick cap. We were taking a shower one day and Buzz finally shaved my head, the last few hairs. It is shocking to see me bald. After he shaved my head, Buzz kept saying how strange it would be to make love to a bald woman – rather exotic. It never ceases to amaze me how the male population can find something sexual in just about any situation. I am definitely pleased he still finds me attractive.

It's surprising how much heat one loses off the top of the head! Along with my wig, I have a good supply of scarves and hats.

Regroup

I am feeling uncomfortable with my relationship with Buzz. We are not fighting, but he is wrapped up in his work, and I am wrapped up in doing what I need to do to heal. Our focus and energies are going in separate directions, and it's difficult to come together. We will set up a time, and then I feel too physically sick or uncomfortable to connect, or we have a time set and Buzz has a business crisis to solve. We need to regroup our efforts and set aside time for one another. I'm concerned, because he doesn't have anyone to talk with, or maybe he simply doesn't want to talk about it. Tonight, he is going out to dinner with his good friend, Mike. I am glad Buzz will have an opportunity to share. The emotional body can only hold so much before there is an explosion.

Gratitude Exercise

What am I grateful for today? Having the energy to buy cotton to crochet trim on a pillowcase for a Christmas present. Too tired to actually figure out the pattern and crochet, I watched a movie while putting together some small decorative cardboard boxes. I am grateful for feeling a little more organized and using my creativity.

I felt least grateful for having to tell a coworker I could not write an evaluation for a former client that she took on due to me taking a leave of absence. She would have to find someone else or wait until I felt better. I didn't feel comfortable saying no, but a part of me was relieved and felt good about me saying no!

Cancer is teaching me about a very prominent archetype (a universal pattern of behavior) found in many people who are in the helping professions: the rescuer. Being a rescuer is a great gift and blessing for many people. However, I need to practice saying 'no.' I can't fix and rescue everyone. I am learning to say, "Let me think about this and get back to you" without feeling the need to provide a lengthy explanation.

Prayer Meeting

Buzz and I decided to have a family prayer session with our daughter, Alyce, instead of going to church (the boys and Mindy were not home.) I did not have the energy to respond to the question "How are you?" from the kind people at church. We opened with a prayer and read Scripture. It was meaningful and healing for me. We talked about cancer and how it was affecting us. Alyce has a wonderful attitude. She said, "Why dwell on fears that aren't even here? What is there to be frightened about in this moment?"

Buzz shared the frustrations and stress he faces daily trying to balance tending to me, to his children, to his work, to financial issues. Alyce brought to his attention that sometimes he comes home and displaces some of that frustration on her. I then tried to explain how weak I feel and how difficult it is to expel the extra energy to be more patient with everyone.

Because we experienced a deeper level of understanding, our love and patience levels were expanded considerably. I feel happy and hopeful about this Christmas, the birth of Christ.

As I prepare myself, as we all prepare ourselves, we will experience Christ's birth in our hearts.

Death

It has been three days since the 2nd chemo injection. I am armed and ready with medications to offset the side effects of CHOP. So far, all is well. Mentally, this second round has been tougher to face. I feel anxious, guarded, scared, and overwhelmed.

As I talked with my sister, Corinne, last night, something important sunk deeper into my spirit. We talked about wasting precious energy thinking about death, or when a person will die. It's going to happen to all of us. Somehow it made sense for me to stop ruminating about death and move on with life, and yet, there is a voice inside that keeps urging me to look at death – *my* death, instead of pretending that death only happens to other people.

Anna

This last week I have felt wonderful – very tired in the afternoons, but no other side effects. Abby and I went to the flea market in honor of her birthday. It was a sunny day, but cold. How wonderful to go several hours without thinking of cancer.

Laurie called me tonight and shared the news that Anna, a friend of hers, had died. I had only met Anna once, but I felt terrible. She died of an advanced case of breast cancer, leaving a husband and three young children. At first, Laurie didn't want to tell me, but didn't want me to hear the news secondhand, either. I think to myself, *why wouldn't she want to tell me this news? I'm not like this woman. I'm different. I don't have the horrible cancer she has!* As the evening wore on, a heaviness descended as I realized, *I could be this woman. If I listen to the voice of Dr. Death, do I have five years, ten years? How much time do I have?*

Laurie said that Anna did not seem prepared for death. In fact, a week before she died, she seemed surprised she was so sick. Anna was very frightened to die. Thinking about Anna's fear of death makes me sad, but, even with my faith, I am frightened, too. Not so much of actually dying, as I know there are plenty of drugs for pain, but of death itself, facing the unknown. Thinking of her three small children brought tears, lots of them. I think about leaving my children. I might never see them married or meet my grandchildren. It's too much to think about. There is no point in thinking about it. I believe God is just and somehow God will balance the scales, but not to be prepared for death? I can't imagine—but then, I'm prepared for everything. Laurie wants to borrow my good china and silver for the funeral luncheon, which I am happy to loan her. I wonder if I should offer to help.

No, I just can't.

Death Thoughts

I have begun to think about my funeral and my desire to be prepared, as a gift of love for my family. No heavy decisions for my family to make. I will have it all written down. Once again, I feel the struggle within: If I actually prepare for death emotionally, physically and spiritually, will death find me? Amy Harwell's words in her book, *Ready to Live, Prepared to Die,* keep coming back to me. She said, "I had worked through my dying to go on with my living. I believe that once we have prepared to die, we are really freed to live in whatever time we have left." Her message makes sense to me. However, I don't think I can make the physical preparation until I have faced my fear of death. Strangely, I go back and forth like a yo-yo, feeling God close to me, feeling completely safe, and then, at times, terrified.

I turned to Hafiz once again for his wisdom, *"Death is a favor to us, but our scales have lost their balance. The impermanence of the body should give us great clarity, deepening the wonder in our senses and eyes... Death is a favor to us, but our minds have lost their balance. The miraculous existence and impermanence of form always makes the illumined ones laugh and sing.*

Chapter 7 – Death

"When death is denied, life loses its depth.
The possibility of knowing who we are beyond name and form,
the dimension of the transcendent, disappears from our lives
because death is the opening into that dimension."
~Eckhart Tolle

Shortly after hearing about the death of Anna, I had lunch with Donna, someone I had never actually met. We shared the same oncologist and were receiving the identical cancer protocol. Realizing we lived in the same town, and with Donna's permission, my oncologist gave me her name. I called her and we met for lunch. Donna was an attractive, thirty-five-year-old career woman, married with no children. After sharing our experiences with the diagnosis and how we were tolerating chemotherapy, Donna said in a very certain voice, "I really don't expect to live past fifty."

In a halting voice, I responded, "I will be fifty next year." Her words shocked me. I suppressed a desire to scream at her to take back those words before her body *heard*. I did not feel I knew her well enough to go into a lengthy explanation about the strong connection between the body, mind and spirit.

Like most who live in the Western Hemisphere, death was something I had no interest in exploring. However, upon returning home, I decided I would no longer hide my head at the mention of death and dying. I made a decision to look at death, *my* death. Sharing this desire with my woman's prayer group, the consensus was they were open to discussing death. Even then, I could sense the fear in their eyes and I realized this is not a topic you can discuss freely in Western society. There are many taboos, restrictions, and negatives about death. It seems strange. The main message of the Christian faith is the resurrection, of life after death. Isn't death something we could be talking about with some anticipation and excitement? I made up my mind. This was a journey I would take.

After the third round of chemotherapy, when I felt physically stronger, and psychologically encouraged I had approached the halfway mark of treatment I wrote about 'facing my fear of death.'

Journal Entries –

Facing death – November 1995

It is now November – what an appropriate time to study death. The leaves are lying in puddles at the feet of all the trees. I can see their imperfections, the misshapen limbs, the holes in the bark, the leaning trunks.

They are all naked – like me. I am stripped of everything. My body hair is gone. I have no energy, no appetite, no motivation to do anything. My masks are gone. I am stuck with me and my fearful thoughts.

What is death to me?

Death is the end. The door is closed. The unknown, darkness, night, alone. This part of me feels terrified. On the other hand, Death is a new birth, a new beginning, another door opens. Excitement, anticipation, wonder. This is the part that feels God's love at a knowing place.

Why do people die?

It seems the natural order of belonging to the earth, to make room for the new. Death is a part of this earthly life. God's design. My faith tells me there is a plan for me, for us all. I can only trust that God sees a larger picture. God must love us a great deal to have designed death. Perhaps it is to draw us closer in a spiritual plane unavailable to us on earth – the next step to our evolving into our true self, the person God created us to be.

What happens when we die?

I believe Jesus will come to me with all the people who have loved me and died: Dad, Mimi, Paw Paw, my Grandfather, Grandmother, Aunt Sophie.

I will be welcomed into heaven, which consists of 'many mansions.' I will learn and grow spiritually in heaven. I am so oriented into 'doing' I can't conceive of doing nothing for eternity. Maybe my first task will be to finish loving myself and 'do' nothing!

My friends believe in reincarnation. I don't know. If God wants me to return to the earth to perfect my soul, so be it. The earth is achingly beautiful, heaven must be comparable. A part of me questions whether there is anything at all after death, perhaps a void, nothingness.

How do I feel about my own death?

A very large part of me feels, sad, scared, alone, and worried about the loved ones I would leave behind. Incredulously, my worst fear, a cancer diagnosis, with no known cure, has come true. I feel shocked and surprised, angry, gypped and short-changed that I have to deal with death now, when I am not even 50 years old. Another part feels excited, as I embark on a new journey. Everyone is terminal. We must all take this journey to death and beyond. The difficult part is living in a society that behaves as if death is not a normal part of life. Many people will take this journey unprepared. My deepest desire was to make friends with death and to be prepared for the journey.

What are my first memories about death?

The first memory was a conversation with Mom in the kitchen at the age of six or seven. My teacher had read a children's book in school called 'The Good Little Angel' about a young child that had died and became an angel. This little angel wandered around heaven with no mother or father, not quite fitting in and having no direction. I was curious, and little afraid of heaven, so I asked, "Mom, where do you go after you die? Can you have ice cream there?" She responded, "Of course you can."

Mom went on to describe heaven as an idyllic place, a sense of being with God and not necessarily doing anything. I was happy about the ice cream, but even then a feeling of intense boredom swept over me at the idea of doing nothing and a fear of being alone in a strange place.

Another memory washed over me. The summer before I was to begin high school, my grandfather (Paw Paw) died. Mom matter-of-factly announced to all of us at dinner, "Children, Paw Paw died today. I am going to Springfield tomorrow to help plan for the funeral. I will be gone for a week. I expect you older children to help with the younger kids and to help Dad with the concession stand at the Quarry."

The Quarry was the local swimming pool and Dad ran the concession stand during the summer to make extra money. He could not leave. Paw Paw was Mom's father and she showed no overt sadness, no display of emotion, no tears, and no hugs for us. Dad looked sad, but no tears. Mom left for the funeral alone. There was no mention of me or my siblings attending. I felt sad and pained over this loss. I loved my Grandfather, who had a droll sense of humor, calling my two younger brothers, "The Jones Boys," to hear us exclaim, "Paw Paw, that's not their name!" He would laugh and tell funny stories.

Death did not seem important to Dad or Mom. I was not given 'permission' to cry or grieve for Paw Paw. Mom was gone for a week and upon her return asked if I would stay in Springfield with Grandmother for a while, as she was lonely. I was thirteen and reluctant to go by myself. I had never gone far away alone, however, I agreed to go. I wondered what would I do with Grandmother? Quiet and reserved by nature, in the time I was with her, she rarely spoke. Her grief and sadness were palpable, but never shared. I was lonely. She would not allow me to watch TV, other than news programs. I remembered I needed deodorant for the first time and feeling embarrassed to ask her. Thankfully, I met some young people my age down the street who invited me to go swimming. Even with her hair in fat curlers, sitting and sunning in an inner tube, one of the girls looked cute and confident, laughing and talking to her friends. I felt the agonizing, adolescent pain of not fitting in – that utter loneliness of not belonging.

After two weeks, I finally went home. Soaking in Grandmother's pain and grief, I felt abandoned by my Mother to 'take care' of my Grandmother and did not have a clue how to help her. Paw Paw's death was never discussed after that.

Years later, my mother shared with me how surprised she was that she never shed any tears when Paw Paw died. She shrugged her shoulders as if to say 'how strange.' And then added, "We were never close."

Visualization

Cathy, my friend who is helping me explore my angst about dying and leaving my loved ones, just left. She read a meditation/visualization. As she read the meditation, I felt intense loss centered in my chest, like tight bands. I could feel Jesus' presence, and, because I love to dance, in my mind's eye I began to dance this loss, sadness, and grief while Jesus sat and watched me. After I finished, I placed my head in his lap and he comforted me. He then watched as I 'sculpted' the feeling of loss using clay. Soft, smooth, and wet, I could feel the clay and began to fashion a vase.  *Unfinished, without the glaze, I felt certain Buzz could finish it easily, as he could finish raising the children. Cathy said she envisioned me dancing with small children in a field and the message was, 'fear not, little one' – that Jesus was addressing the fears of the child in me who grew up with fears of death and dying, and being alone or abandoned.*

I felt God's presence today. A healing took place. I have been given courage to move forward in my journey to prepare myself for death, so I can put my energy into living.

Insights and experiences of other people gave me the strength and courage to pursue this topic. I continued to read about death and the dying process, near-death experiences, and how to be with someone who is dying.

One night I woke up with my heart pounding. Once again, I was filled with fear of dying. Is there anything after death? What if all I had been taught as a child about God and heaven was not true? I suddenly remembered a small children's book called, Emma Says Goodbye, by Carolyn Nystrom, a local Christian author. In my years of wallpapering and painting as a business for other people, before I returned to school for my Master's in Social Work, I had done work for Carolyn, and she had given me several of her books. I never read 'Emma Says Goodbye,' because in reading the synopsis I saw right away it was about an aunt, who has cancer and dies, and her close relationship with her niece, Emma. I also have a young niece, my Goddaughter, named Emma. In my fear of death, I actually hid the book behind the bookcase in my bedroom and until this night had forgotten about it.

After pulling it out from behind the bookcase, I crawled back into bed and began to read. Written from a Christian perspective, the story was beautiful. The author talked about life as mystery, "Why do people die when their loved ones have prayed that the person will be healed? Why doesn't God always answer our prayers? Why is there suffering? Who has the answers for these questions?" So, we turn to our faith in God – our faith that God will never leave us – that nothing, neither life, nor death, can separate us from God's love. I then remembered something I had read, which was a Buddhist perspective about this question of life after death. The author posed the question: "How is it possible for something to turn into nothing?" He went on to state, "It is impossible. Look at creation. Nothing dies, it is simply transformed."

I put the book down and noticed moonlight streaming in through the bedroom window. Slipping out of bed, I wrapped myself in a blanket and sat in a chair by the window. As  *I soaked in the moonlight and stared at the moon, I thought about the perfect order of Nature. In the Midwest, the four seasons are acutely evident. They come and go in all their glory and with each change of season death and rebirth are always present whether you are an insect, plant or animal. Why should it be any different for humans? Suddenly, I knew that if death were a 'normal' part of Nature, then all would be well with death for anyone on the planet, including me. Death was the natural consequence of created living entities.*

With this simple insight the panicked fear of death left me.

Over the years, Nature has continued to teach me other cherished lessons about death: what we think is dead might only be sleeping, resting, or growing stronger waiting until the right moment to blossom, and perhaps a death is needed to re-birth into a renewed, transformed life.

While walking in the small woods on my property with several of the women from my spirituality group, six years after cancer treatment, I noticed something I had never seen before. Standing in front of me was a large tree that had split and fallen into the arms of three smaller trees. This had happened quite some time ago, because the branches of the three smaller trees had actually wrapped or grown their branches around the collapsed trunk. The fallen tree looked dead. I walked closer to the tree and saw nubile buds waiting to open on the branches.

The tree was not dead.

I followed the line of the tree and saw that it was barely connected to the main tree truck, but enough to sustain life.

With tears rolling down my cheeks I saw myself after the cancer diagnosis as the fallen tree barely holding on – with God, my friends and family as the three smaller trees holding me. In that moment, the memories of that time, all the suffering flooded back with an indescribable sweetness – because it was the suffering that produced the spiritual and emotional growth that truly transformed me. And so, when the gardens and woods were open to the public several years later, that part of the woods became known as Surrender. Not giving up but surrendering to what is in this present moment – with the knowledge of the universal truth, 'All is well.' This special place also reminds me that I am, that we all are God's hands on this earth helping one another live and when the time comes – we will help each other rebirth into a new life. In a message from God, Saint Mechtilde heard: *"Do not fear your death. For when that moment comes, I will draw in my breath and your soul will come to me like a needle to a magnet."*

Chapter 8 – Treatment Continues

"...in any situation in life, confronted by an outer threat or opportunity, you can notice yourself responding inwardly in one of two ways. Either you will brace, harden and resist, or you will soften, open and yield. If you go with the former gesture, you will be catapulted immediately into your smaller self, with its animal instincts and survival responses. If you stay with the latter ... you will remain in alignment with your innermost being and through it, divine being can reach you."
~Cynthia Bourgeault

Going into the fourth round of chemotherapy, I felt rebellious. Rebellious in the sense that I was sick of this illness. I didn't want to talk about it anymore, pray about it anymore, or meditate about it anymore. I was sick of taking the herbs, sick of making teas, sick of being sick and tired! After each round of chemotherapy, I experienced a low-grade fever. Each time I was prepared with a strong antibiotic, but it was difficult to function with a constant fever and low white counts. Every move was an effort. While grocery shopping, I needed to hang onto a shopping cart for support, sometimes I just left the store, went home and crawled back into bed. I felt I was hanging on by a thread. My body was fighting very hard as each round left me more and more fatigued.

With my energy levels falling to an alarming level, I was grateful beyond words for any assistance. Meals, prayers, cards, and encouragement kept coming from family and friends, which were a lifeline for me, especially going into the Christmas season.

Every Christmas season decorating the tree was a family function with Christmas music softly playing, logs cracking in the fireplace and camaraderie. However, this year, everyone seemed to have other plans. My son announced he was leaving early to go hunting. My oldest daughter said she had to work. My youngest daughter wanted to go horseback riding with a friend. And my husband said he had an appointment with a client. I was irritated and disappointed. During dinner, with a deep sigh, I asked them, "Isn't a decorated tree important to you? Don't you see I do not have the energy to do this myself?" They all said they would help on another day. However, I wanted them to have the same excitement and understand how important this was to me. Deep inside I wondered if this was the end of this tradition as a family – that I might not live to experience another Christmas. Those thoughts were too horrific to share.

Thanks to my sister, Ann, who was in town for a visit offered to help me decorate the tree. Ann has a creative enthusiastic flair for decorating anything. It was fun listening to her ideas and trying something new! Having this task completed gave me a sense of normalcy and peace.

Later that week, while waiting outside for Mindy to finish her horseback riding lesson at the riding school, I began a casual conversation with the father of another young rider. We were leaning against the fence that surrounded the paddock. The air was brisk and cool with heavy thick clouds overhead. The forecast had predicted the first snowfall of the year, which I was happily anticipating. After talking about the soon arrival of the Christmas rush, the conversation shifted. I could feel my body tensing, as he shared, "I really feel sad and concerned. A good friend of mine has cancer and is not doing very well."

A hard rock began to form in my stomach. Trying to sound calm, I asked him, "What kind of cancer does he have?"

"Non-Hodgkin's lymphoma," he replied, and went on to say, "My friend went through chemotherapy and the cancer has now come back seven years later. It is touch and go. It doesn't look like he's going to make it."

I mumbled some sympathetic comment and then quickly added, "I'm really cold. I think I will wait in the car." Sitting in the car, with my head resting on the steering wheel I felt cold to the bone and could not stop shaking. I did not share with this man that I had the same cancer. As I listened to the story about his friend, the familiar panic settled in – Dr. Death's words screaming in my head: *You have five to seven years to live.*

When I returned home, I was able to share what happened with Buzz, and gain some perspective. Covering my cold hands with his warm touch and focusing his soft brown eyes on mine in a gentle, but firm tone, he reminded me, "You know nothing about this man's friend, what kind of lymphoma, what stage, what his lifestyle is, and what kind of treatment he chose."

I began to calm down and saw how quickly I jumped right into the 'what-if' mode of thinking. Dr. Death's prognosis was only his opinion, and not truth, and yet, I allowed his words to take my peace of mind. I vowed never again to give those words – *You have five to seven years to live,* so much power.

After our conversation, later that night, we made love. Buzz knew me well and could read my thoughts without my saying anything. He only needed to look at my tense body and face to see the fear still lurking from my earlier encounter. He warmed a jar of scented body oil and proceeded to give me an oil massage. With each tender stroke the fear and tenseness melted. I have lost almost all body hair and making love seems a strange experience. It was warm and loving. I felt like a woman again, not this strange-looking alien – Buzz and the children never say anything about how I look. I see myself in this goofy scarf and I wonder, *who is this person?*

I could not sleep at night. My mind kept racing with fearful thoughts. I fell back into the whirlpool of negative thoughts about the possible outcome of this disease that Buzz had recently talked me through. I needed something tangible in bed to hold or to touch that reminded me of God's presence. Holding the Bible on my chest or a wooden cross helped, but I would wake up soon after falling asleep. I put out an SOS for a stuffed lamb, which I thought would remind me of God's love, that all is well. Soon after, Mary, my mother-in-law, sent me a precious, soft lamb, about twelve inches tall and stuffed with beans. He just molded to my body. It was the sweetest little lamb. Holding it gave me pleasure and comfort. I did not have stuffed toys as a child and never thought of them as having value. However, with this lamb, the

little girl who resided in me, lost and hidden was now being fed, recognized and comforted. In doing so she became a powerful ally on my path to healing with her spontaneous, fun loving, child-like, trusting nature.

As a child growing up, my siblings and I would take turns lighting a candle on the Advent wreath and opening a small door on the Advent calendar to mark the four weeks before Christmas. Every week we would light another candle until by the fourth week all four candles were lit around the wreath. As Christmas Eve drew closer, we all tried to guess who would have the great fortune to open the last door revealing the crèche scene. We were giddy with excitement.

Buzz and I continued this Advent tradition. Every evening before dinner we lit a candle on the Advent wreath, and Mindy, our youngest, would read a prayer. At the end of the prayer, we would all say, "Come, Lord Jesus." One night when I heard the prayer, I knew *the Lord Jesus had come in the form of this little stuffed lamb.* Simply holding the lamb salved the scars in me and calmed my fears. I felt safe. Buzz understood my angst and was delighted to have anything help calm my fearful ruminations. As a child, Mindy understood perfectly the value of a stuffed animal and during dinner one evening asked me, "What is his name?" Buzz, with his witty sense of humor immediately christened the lamb Jesús (hay-soos), the Spanish name for Jesus.

Several weeks later, I attended an Advent prayer service at the Cenacle retreat house. While waiting for the program to begin I noticed the leader walking up the aisle with a framed picture in her hand. On the table by the lectern. she placed a large picture of Jesus, tenderly holding a lamb. My heart stopped. As I looked at the picture, I felt Jesus holding me.

In tears, I asked her to make a copy of the picture for me. After lunch she handed me a copy, with a rather pale and faded print, but I was happy. Soon after, as I walked by a local bookstore, I saw the same picture, propped on an easel in the window. With my heart pounding, I went inside and bought a perfect print for just five dollars! I wondered who is this Mother/Father God that loves me this much to provide another beacon of light in this terrifying cancer journey?

Was this all coincidence or a synchronistic happening?

Some people feel synchronicity is only selective perception, or the law of averages playing itself out or simply random coincidence. Carl Jung believed synchronicity was a glimpse into the underlying order of the universe. He coined the term *synchronicity* to describe a *meaningful* coincidence of outer and inner events that are connected and cannot be explained by cause and effect. For me, synchronistic happenings are kisses or hugs from God, letting us know that life is full of mystery and surprise. And that, no matter what, 'all is well.' It is important we keep our eyes open and senses honed, to receive and recognize synchronistic events, as they are vital beacons of light to guide us. I found that when I let go of control, constantly thinking about how to solve this or that, I could move into a heart space of prayer, surrendering to the hand of God, resting in God. Synchronicities became a common occurrence showing me I am not alone.

After the fourth round of chemotherapy, when I was sick again with a fever and stomach problems, I went to see my Chinese herbalist. He gave me herbs for my stomach, which made me feel much better. It's amazing how I could be watching television or reading, and all of a sudden, realize I no longer hurt. It's such a wonderful feeling. I discovered that sometimes I could get so used to pain that it took time for me to realize the pain was gone.

My experience of our Christmas Eve celebration was very different this year. I felt like an observer rather than a participant in the celebration. I felt detached, yet, it was lovely being around family and friends. I wore my wig, which scratched my head. I missed Dad who had died the year before in January 1995, six months before I was diagnosed with cancer. I put together a short memorial service, and shared it with my family that night. We were all thinking about Dad, as this was our first Christmas without him. We joined together in mourning Dad's loss in gratitude for the gift of his life.

Also, that evening, a relative who struggles with depression, arrived late. He definitely started the Christmas party early as he could barely walk. In talking with him that evening, for the first time I felt a deep empathy and understanding of his pain. He sounded suicidal in his loneliness, like he was in a deep cavern with no exit, paradoxically, in the middle of this huge, boisterous family. I was both impressed and surprised when he called me the next day to apologize for having too much to drink. Perhaps, he appreciated my non-judgmental, empathic response to him and that I could recognize his suffering. I quietly noted that on this cancer journey my heart was opening in a more spacious, compassionate way to imperfections we all have in this human family.

On the other hand, Christmas Day itself, with Buzz and our children, was wonderful. There was no screaming or yelling. Everyone was patient and sweet and enjoyed sharing and opening their gifts. Buzz and I watched movies all day and slept. However, the next day, the Christmas blues soon settled over me. I wrote in my journal:

I am struggling with depression, perhaps a combination of the letdown after the excitement of the Christmas preparations and the side effects of chemotherapy – feeling like a prisoner in my own body. After the last chemotherapy, there was no physical pain in my stomach, or bowel dysfunction, just an incredible weakness. It took effort to turn a page in a book, so I was forced to do nothing, but read, watch TV, or observe the animals outside. Today is a typical January day – cold, cloudy, and gray. I feel like a wet noodle, no energy. It's hard to walk. It's even hard to think. I knew this last part of treatment would be the most difficult psychologically. It is one thing not to feel good on a sunny fall day and another not to feel good on a gray, cold, January day.

Several weeks later, with Buzz's blessing and support, I decided not to go back to work full-time. I needed time to heal. The part-time person agreed to take my place full-time. I wondered again, *where will this cancer journey take me?*

I applied for Social Security Disability, which we hoped would help us pay for our expensive health insurance. Being self-employed and paying for insurance was a heavy financial burden, something Buzz felt every day. It seemed as if Buzz and I had stepped off a cliff into a dark abyss. We were falling, and didn't know where, or how, we would land financially.

Applying for SS Disability was labor-intensive and overwhelming. It was humbling to ask for help. It seemed we had failed in some way. There were volumes of papers to fill out. It was unnerving. I had to see, and document in black and white, that there was no known cure for my type of lymphoma. Oh, and that we had no money to pay for medical insurance, because we are self-employed.

One evening, I watched *Lifeboat*, an old movie about shipwrecked people who found themselves drifting at sea. For a long period of time, they didn't know where they were going, or whether they would live or die. As they were floating with no food or drinking water, I could feel what that would be like. After watching the movie, I decided to lie on our waterbed, visualizing floating and questioning: *Where am I going? Where is my health going? Where is my profession going? Where is my life going?* I rather enjoyed the waves.

Feeling calm and collected after the 'boat ride' in our waterbed, I pumped up my pillows and continued to read a wonderful book by Larry Dossey, MD, called *Healing Words*. He documented all the scientific experiments done on the effectiveness of prayer. In the book, Dossey tells the story of a young man who is in a blinding snowstorm in Antarctica. He is camping with a group of people and ventures outside to feed the dogs. Even though they have put stakes in the ground as guides, he can't see them and becomes disoriented, and lost. He knows if he continues to walk, he will die; so, he digs a hole in the snow and hunkers down. He tells himself to *relax and try to enjoy this*. Thirteen hours later, he was found. He said it felt like he was in his mother's womb and he could feel his heartbeat. He could feel his smallness, next to the Antarctic, and he could sense the *essence* of Antarctica.

Dossey's words to settle down and enjoy the experience overwhelmed me. The fact that the young man did not fight the storm, but relaxed and surrendered to the present moment. What an extraordinary idea, really, to settle down and enjoy the cancer ride!

In thinking about this young man's experience using Nature as a container and surrendering to the present moment, a memory surfaced – that of the rock quarry. Every summer for eighteen years, my father ran the concession stand at the quarry, which served as the local swimming pool. Dad's real job was as school superintendent in a district forty minutes away. But during the summers, he was a 'peanuts-and-popcorn' man, loving the interaction with all who came to the concession stand, especially the children. All of my siblings and I were expected to work there. Often, we rode our bikes down the blacktopped, steep drive that took us to the bottom of the hills surrounding the quarry pool. I can still close my eyes and remember the exhilarating experience of flying down the hills, the smell of the musty woods, the coolness of the breeze against my body, my long hair flying behind me. The anxiety of wiping out on some errant stone under my bike tire was always present, but I chose the joy of the ride over the fear.

Later in the day, the hills around the quarry became the African jungle as Ann, KT (a childhood friend), and I played Tarzan, Jane and Boy. While swinging from thick grapevines hanging from the trees, we screamed the Tarzan yell, and escaped from villains. Those times in Nature, I was immersed in present moment time – God's time.

Now, as an adult on this scary, perilous journey I was calling back the little girl in me who chose joy of life over fear. I felt I was beginning to make a slow, gentle shift to become more conscious of the blessings that each day brings and start experiencing the wisdom and grace of present moment mindfulness. One day, just looking out the window, I noticed how I was enjoying watching the variety of birds at the feeder, and the squirrels that were trying so hard to feast on the seed. I found myself thinking how I couldn't wait until spring. In mid-thought I stopped myself, knowing I didn't want to go there. *I didn't want to miss today and what today had to bring.* I was pleased with myself for catching that rushed thought, making the decision to stay in the present moment. But then, I suddenly realized that in a split second I allowed myself to consider I might live to see spring. What an exciting moment.

The last round of treatment was approaching. It felt as if I was in the last five miles of a hideous marathon run. Just completing simple tasks required a titanic effort. For the last several weeks, I have been experiencing hot flashes. Chemotherapy catapulted me into menopause. I went from one month having regular periods to the next month having none. While I watched TV, the hot flashes came every thirty minutes. During the night, they occurred about every forty-five minutes. I would wake up drenched in sweat, throw off the covers, and within several minutes be cold. Sleeping was a challenge. The doctors told me I couldn't have any estrogen until treatment was completed. *Will I continue with menopause after the treatment is over? Will my periods return?* Nobody seems to know. *Should I do hormone-*

replacement therapy after chemotherapy? Due to the intense side effects of menopause, I decided I would take hormone-replacement therapy after treatment was over. It was a decision I later regretted.

We found out we would soon have to start paying $700 a month for my health insurance, an astronomical amount for us. Laurie suggested I should explore every avenue. She said that with all our medical bills, we might qualify for public assistance. What a sobering thought. I had often recommended to my clients that they apply for public aid before we accepted them into the drug program. They would receive a medical card that would pay for their treatment. Now, I felt embarrassed, ashamed and angry that it was necessary for me to go down the same path.

On the day I applied, a sweet Hispanic woman at the public assistance office helped me gather all the forms. She told me about a woman with cancer who had come into her office. She had prayed for this woman, and later, was told all the cancer was gone. I asked her to pray for me. She said she would. I told my sister, "How wonderful, *God's Golden Web.* I have someone else praying for me, just when I detested the thought of walking into her office." After gathering an incredible amount of information, I was told we did not qualify for public aid. I was disappointed, yet relieved. *We were not considered poor enough*

Cancer is a humbling experience.

Cathy was going to take me to see Dr. Carolyn Myss the next day. Myss is a pioneer in the field of energy medicine and a popular speaker on spirituality and personal power. I knew before I went that I was meant to be there to receive information to help me heal. I was not disappointed.

At the workshop, Carolyn Myss shared some of the content of her new book, *Anatomy of the Spirit.* She said, "Our

131

biography becomes our biology." Certain negative messages and beliefs we hold to be true about ourselves can cause emotional stress and affect how we respond to life – and can develop into illness. Her ideas were a tremendous help for me. She confirmed what I knew to be true and gave me tools to become more conscious. I knew I had to look deeper into myself. There was fear and trepidation along with the excitement of knowing her information would help me heal. Feeling stronger, I journaled my thoughts:

> *Carolyn Myss presented the workshop along with Ron Roth, an ex-priest and healer. Ron talked about people coming to his healing services and not wanting to be healed because they were receiving too many benefits from being sick. It reminded me of Bernie Siegel's question that I pondered when I was first diagnosed, "Why do you need your illness and what benefits do you derive from it?" I was disturbed to think I still might need this disease; knowing those thoughts would keep me from a complete healing. I remembered my therapist, when I was beginning this journey, telling me not voicing those feelings is what is dangerous, everyone gets something out of being sick. There are perks in being sick. I want to focus my energy on wellness, not on having cancer. I wish to move forward with ascension-thinking and transcending cancer.*

An opportunity arose for me to attend an *anointing of the sick*, a special service at church, and I decided to attend. There was a modest attendance that cold evening in January. I chose a seat in the middle of the church and shyly looked around wondering what ailment brought each person. *Coming here takes courage,* I thought. No one in this society likes to be signaled out as different or in need of help. When the invitation was given for all those people who desired healing to come forward to be blessed by the priest, I hesitated for only a moment, then stepped forward. My prayer intention was focused on discarding any 'holding on' to the cancer for whatever benefits being sick could bring, such as, martyrdom, imagining people commenting on how courageous I am. I do not need an illness to feel loved or to build my self-esteem. After the healing service I felt light and free.

Lent was approaching and I decided to ask God to open my eyes to any blindness in me. Sometimes one had better be careful what one asks for – because you just might get it.

- I noticed a spiritual pride. I have read more spiritual books, studied scripture, attended more retreats, and developed a meditation practice, therefore, I considered myself more knowledgeable about spiritual matters.
- I noticed a judgmental attitude toward people who do not have the same understanding that I have about life and pursuing what I feel is the 'correct way' to handle finances, child rearing, illness, relationships and some life issues.
- I noticed a lack of trust in God concerning finances, and my health, which is rooted in fear.

My image of God was changing. In past years, I have studied parts of the Bible, but never read it from cover to cover. Ever since the diagnosis I became determined to read parts of the Old Testament, and then a Psalm and end with a New Testament reading, slowly reading through the Bible chronologically. Surprisingly, I discovered a loving Father

God in the Old Testament, a Father who forgives his stiff-necked, stubborn, beloved people over and over. Shortly after reading most of the Old Testament, I experienced a healing in my relationship with God. It was as if, in a single moment, the immature, hell and damnation fears taught to me as a child about God completely disappeared.

Up to this point in my life, I only saw Jesus as accessible. I prayed with a vivid picture of Jesus holding me, walking with me, resting with me, dancing with me. God, the Father, was not.

One day, after my Centering Prayer practice, I was sitting with my eyes still closed in silence. In my imagination, I suddenly saw an elderly man sitting on a huge stone throne. I was very small in comparison, like a child. I haltingly asked, "Are you my Father God?"

He nodded, yes.

Fearful, I asked another question, "Are you the God of Moses and Abraham?" I was afraid because the God of the Old Testament, the same fearsome God of my childhood, was very strict. He nodded *yes* and then pointed to his knee. Like a child, I climbed up and God held me and loved me with a mother's tenderness. I have never experienced such an all-consuming love – a Father/Mother complete love.

I believe we can read, study, and even quote scripture, but until there is an experience of God all our knowledge of God is like eating dust.

After this experience I thought about my earthly father. I wondered if he had petitioned Father/Mother God to love me in all the ways he could not, as Dad was hurt himself. Later that day, driving into the city with Laurie for my last cancer treatment, I remembered some comforting words from the presenter at a retreat I attended for young mothers years ago. Some of the mothers, myself included, had voiced guilt for not being the perfect mothers we had envisioned before our children were born. He said, "Be grateful you and your children were not loved perfectly, for you would never seek God or need anyone." I remembered that hearing these words for the first time began my healing journey of forgiving my parents for not loving me the way I thought I needed.

As we pulled up in front of the hospital, I once again, prayed that God would fill in the gaps and nurture me. I understood at a deeper level Mom and Dad did the best they could with the love they were given as children. A soft cloud of compassion and love toward my parents enveloped me.

Chapter 9 – Treatment Is Over, Now What?

"We do not grow absolutely, chronologically. We grow sometimes in one dimension, and not in another – unevenly. We grow partially. We are relative. We are mature in one realm, childish in another. The past, present and future mingle and pull us backward, forward, or fix us in the present. We are made up of layers, cells, constellations."
~Anais Nin

Six weeks after my last treatment, with winter almost over, a recurring thought occupied my mind. Now that treatment was over, and my hair was growing back, the cancer could come back, too. The 'protective wall' was gone. *How do I live with the threat of cancer returning or popping up some place else in my body?* I ruminated about the leftover toxic effects of the chemotherapy. *Will another condition present itself down the road?* Scared, but relieved there was no more treatment, the cancer journey continued with the removal of the porta-cath. Painful and sore, it felt like a stab wound. I journaled:

I feel restless and lonely tonight. Buzz has been working long hours and falls asleep on the couch for the night. Questions and concerns flood my mind. Was it too soon to remove the porta-cath? Will the cancer come back? If it does, will chemotherapy again be an option? I wanted the porta-cath out of me to give me a sense of finality – that I am healed. I wanted to scream at the Doctor, 'Just get this thing out of me! I don't need this anymore! I don't need any more chemo injections!' Now that it is removed comes the thought that I might have to face this journey again. Lately I cry often. I do not know why. Is it relief that I am in remission? Is it menopausal? Fear the cancer will return? Financial concerns? Ever since the completion of chemotherapy, I have been spiraling into a depression.

My depression was deep. I could not write in my journal for weeks. I could barely get dressed, dragging myself through each day trying to stay involved with my family responsibilities and feeling guilty that all I wanted to do was hide. However, every morning I 'showed up' for my twenty minutes of Centering Prayer, which had sustained me during this cancer journey. Two years prior to the diagnosis, I attended a workshop to learn how to practice this type of prayer. Centering Prayer, a method of praying based on the ancient teachings of the Christian Contemplative Tradition, is a prayer of silence. That of resting in God where one opens the mind and heart – one's whole being – to God beyond thoughts, words and emotions. In this deeply stilling form of prayer one chooses a sacred word as the symbol of the intention to consent to God's presence and action within. When thoughts are distracting, which will happen, the idea is to gently return to the sacred word to remember the intention to consent to God's presence, however it is manifested.

My initial reaction to this type of prayer was 'No way can I do this!' For a while after the workshop, I did try praying this way, but I soon gave up convinced it was impossible for me to sit still. I was well aware I was a type A personality, always moving and doing. Because of this, I also knew God was asking me to slow down and learn a way of praying that would teach me how to just *be*.

After the cancer diagnosis, I deeply desired and was highly motivated to learn how to *be*. So, every morning, before my day started, still in my nightgown, sitting in my comfortable bedroom chair by the window facing the woods,

I prepared to enter the silence. I looked at the small items I had carefully selected and placed on the window sill to connect me with God: a small pewter sign that said, 'A new day to celebrate,' given to me by my mother; a small statue of St. Therese of Lisieux, the Saint I chose for my confirmation name; a piece of green beach glass given to me by my son, Nick, to remind me of the beauty of Lake Michigan; a small cross made of olive wood from Jerusalem; a carved statue of the laughing Buddha to remind me to laugh and to remember the Buddhist belief in the impermanence of all things; a small shell from the ocean with five marks, symbolic of the five women with whom I have shared my spiritual journey for twenty years; a flat rock with a carved labyrinth, to represent my journey to God; and, a small acorn to tell me of the magnificent transformation from an acorn to a towering oak tree – and that kind of transformation is available to everyone.

Carefully setting the timer for twenty minutes, I settled into my chair, keeping my spine supported, feet on the floor, hands resting on my lap, eyes closed and silently said my sacred word as a symbol of my consent to God's presence. Gently, I said to myself, 'Abba.' Within seconds, my mind wandered to my 'to do' list of the day and I went through all that still needed to be done. Then I remembered that I was supposed to let go of my thoughts. Quickly, I focused on my sacred word, *Abba*. Soon, another thought took control of my awareness. *Damn! I forgot to return that overdue library book.*

Abba, I silently mouthed again. Then my eye began to twitch, and I thought of how annoying it was.

Abba, I repeated to myself.

Soon, I questioned, *Am I doing this right?*

Oops, another thought.

Abba. I could feel a touch of annoyance. *No, wait, I'm supposed to return to my sacred word gently. Abba.* I wondered, *How much longer?* I peeked at the timer and realized I had been meditating for only three minutes.

Abba, Abba .... My thoughts kept coming, one after the other.

Persevering with this prayer method was difficult and frustrating. However, through reading about the lives of the great Saints, I discovered the importance of staying loyal to the prayer practice whether I liked it or not. It is not the goals set that are important in this prayer practice – spiritual consolations, mystical experiences, making the mind a blank – but rather, a deepening of faith in God's abiding presence, no matter how that manifests itself during the twenty minutes. I was learning another way to surrender. Sometimes I wondered why I bothered. However, I knew that my intention to connect with God and my saying *yes* to God was important whether I felt the connection or not. I kept up the practice and soon discovered the gifts of this prayer method come outside of the twenty minutes, usually much later.

For example, one day, standing in line at the grocery store I became aware that I was not irritated when the person ahead of me had more than twelve items. I was only grateful that I lived in a country that provided such bounty and choices. Later in the week, as I was driving home another driver cut me off. My thought was, *Oh well, that could have been me not paying attention.*

My daily practice of Centering Prayer gently transformed me and gave me the grace and insight to be a loving presence toward the world and myself. I was learning to let go, dramatically aided by the practice of letting go of my thoughts, and returning to the sacred word, and to the present moment. I continued my resolve to become conscious and mindful of my shadow side, that part of me that I did not want to face, by attending another workshop by Dr. Carolyn Myss.

Sitting in a room full of spiritual seekers, Dr. Myss asked, "How many of you want to become conscious, mindful and awake?" We all raised are hands. "Great!" she said and then asked, "What are you willing to do to become conscious, mindful and fully awake? Are you willing to suffer? To undergo loss? Hardship? Illness?"

Everyone was silent.

I've always been aware of choosing to be on a spiritual path, but I would have never chosen the suffering of this cancer as a path to awareness. But here I am. *Welcome to my world, Dr. Myss.*

Lasting, life-changing transformation comes about through some sort of suffering or loss. It is those moments that have the ability to break through deeply engrained thinking patterns from the past that keep us small and afraid.

I began to uncover those negative thinking patterns and negative responses by keeping track of them in a journal, asking myself about my motivation. As soon as I recognized a negative thought toward others, or myself I asked my angels to quickly catch and transform that thought, before it harmed anyone. I was becoming a curious, open, observer of myself, and discovered that awakening to each present moment, without judgment, was where I wanted to be. As I opened myself to becoming more conscious, I saw shadow parts of me that made me cringe. At the same time, I experienced God's love enveloping me. "What a delicious paradox!" Myss would say. Recognizing the deep desire we all have to become conscious, we are often unwilling to suffer for our awareness.

Days later, while sipping herbal tea and opening the mail, I learned I was denied the Social Security Disability I applied for eight weeks earlier. I felt rejected, disappointed, and angry. I cried on and off for three days, grinding over our internal financial struggle. *How will we pay for everything if I am not working? How will I heal if I work?* I shared this news with our friends, Terry and Carmela, who said, "Fight this decision, and reapply. Everyone is denied the first time. You need to hire a disability lawyer." Reluctantly, I contacted Jeff, a disability lawyer, and with his help and guidance, I re-applied.

Several weeks later, I found myself sitting in a psychiatrist's office for a psychological evaluation, in response to a request from the SS Disability Office as part of the application for disability. The doctor asked me kindly, "Why are you here?"

Suddenly, I began sobbing, I could barely speak and finally managed to say, "I had cancer and just finished with chemotherapy. I cannot stop crying. Five different oncologists all told me this cancer had no known cure."

As I was blowing my nose, the doctor told me he wanted to ask me some questions, and to please answer as best I could.

Softly, he asked, "What year is it?"

I thought, *Oh my God, he thinks I'm crazy.* I muttered, "1996."

He proceeded, "Who is the president of the United States?"

My mind went absolutely blank and I could not remember the president's name. However, after a few uncomfortable moments, I did remember and sputtered, "Bill Clinton."

Then he asked, "Who is the Vice President?" and I could not remember. I just shook my head. The doctor then asked me to count backward from 100.

142

Arithmetic was never my strong suit, but in as confident a voice as I could muster, I began, "100, 99, 98, 97, 96, 95, 94, 93, 92, 90, 89." I stopped.

I knew I had forgotten 91. I tried to go back and start over. Finally, I got stuck somewhere around 84 and could not go any further. He then told me the interview was over and that my official diagnosis was 'Adjustment Disorder with Depression.' He prescribed Zoloft, an antidepressant. And then went on to explain, "Often, the neurotransmitter serotonin, the chemical that regulates your mood, becomes depleted in cancer patients who take chemotherapy drugs. It may take a while for the brain to go back to producing the right amount of chemicals."

Even as a therapist in the mental health profession, I felt strange taking an antidepressant. As if I had joined the ranks of the mentally ill, – that somehow, I was marked and couldn't handle my life. The Western belief of *I must pull myself up by my boot straps* was deeply entrenched in modern medicine, as was the assumption there is something wrong with me if I needed help. Another piece of my false pride to let go.

It was spring and with the help of anti-depressants, the veil of darkness lifted. For the last several months, it had not occurred to me I could choose how to face the day. It seemed sadness was my only option. But now, on a lovely spring day, I was able to make a healthy, joyful, exciting decision. After months of observing Nature from a window while I journaled or meditated, a desire to *be* in Nature grew strong. I reasoned that if I could be physically in Nature, the potential for an exciting and meaningful experience was within my reach. I decided to begin this newfound relationship by creating a large, perennial garden with paths, so that at every turn one might be surprised with beauty. Very quickly, Nature fed me thoughts and ideas that helped take me where I wanted to go and opened new paths for me after a long, long time in hibernation!

For Mother's Day, my son, Matt rototilled my chosen area and I began to prepare the soil and plant in earnest. This was the first time I saw myself as an artist using flowers as a palette. Joy filled my spirit as I planted and worked in the garden. I discovered that while I was immersed in the creative process of gardening, I lost all sense of time and my constant companions, Fear and Sadness, were nowhere to be found.

Finally, with my brain neurotransmitters back in balance, the cancer treated and now in the past, I soaked up feeling well and threw myself into the joy of living. I practiced *being*. Wonderful changes were subtly occurring in me through my practice of present moment living. My senses were honed and focused as I worked and created in the garden completely immersed in 'Kairos' time, God's time. In fact, no matter where I went, Nature embraced me. On the beach in Michigan, I journaled:

Before I had cancer, I loved and appreciated Nature. I said, "Thank you, God" at every opportunity. In fact, I prided myself on my 'thank you' status with God. As a cancer survivor, my gratitude has intensified one hundred-fold. Sitting on the beach in Michigan, I am immersed in the warm sun, the soft blue sky and the puffy clouds that slowly drift by. As I look down the beach, watching the shoreline curve around the dunes, there is a soft, ethereal haze that envelops the water. Last night on the beach, watching the fiery ball of sun sink below the horizon, sending out rays of pink and purple light, I could hardly breathe, immersed in that beauty. I have noticed that I no longer look at Nature and say thank you. I look at the sun, sea, and stars and become one with creation – our souls have merged – God, Creation, and Me. A silent, wordless sensation of oneness comes over me.

Chapter 10 – The Rekindling of Desire in Europe

"Love has come to rule and transform.
Stay awake, my heart, stay awake."
~Rumi

The desire was now stronger than ever before to live my life more fully, and before I die, I wanted to be sure and visit some fantastic place with Ann and Laurie. I felt drawn to Europe. Buzz and I had been there on our honeymoon twenty-six years ago. We traveled, we laughed, and we explored the gorgeous, ancient landscape. Looking back, I am now able to see we were too young and did not have the maturity to fully appreciate what we were seeing, just racing from one age-old site to another. The whole idea of honeymooning in Europe was so romantic, but the romance was wasted on me. Being raised as a good Catholic girl, it took me a while into my married life before I could let go of my fear and see the act of sex as being *beautiful and sacred*. I think we missed the depth of the experience all the way around and I wanted another chance at *being* in Europe.

When the idea that I would live through chemo and there would be life after chemo began to manifest, I mentioned to Buzz my desire to take a trip with my sisters and that I was thinking about Europe. We had contacts there and the cost of the trip seemed quite manageable. I asked if he would like to go. He said, "No." Then adding, "I would feel like an intruder in the middle of you and your sisters."

There was something even more obvious, I really needed to get away from everything that reminded me of illness, cancer, struggle, all of it. Was I running away? Maybe.

I really questioned my reasoning, but if I was running from it all, I couldn't think of a better place to run away to. Anyone could call it whatever they wanted, but for me, it was a respite. I knew in my heart I needed to bring back the passion and desire that had been stripped from me through all this illness. I wanted to feel whole again, and I thought Europe may open me to it.

The idea kept fermenting within me. I thought of my two older sisters, and how wonderful it would be to have this experience with them. Even though I knew this was almost impossible, I felt as if I were allowing myself to dream again. Such a feeling of joy. I couldn't help but embrace the idea. I had never gone anywhere with my sisters, and the more I dreamed, the more excited I got.

At times, the 'financial reality check' would jump up in my face and poke a large hole in my dream. I watched as the costs of alternative treatments kept building up on our charge cards, and, to be honest, I did not hold much hope of going.

Three years before, while studying for my Master's Degree, I had attended a week-long intensive dealing with 'family of origin' issues. During the week, the participants shared in small group settings and worked at letting go of childhood hurts and bitter disappointments through journaling, counseling, and the telling of our story. I was impressed with Jim, one of the participants in my group who came all the way to America from London to deal with his family of origin – to recognize negative patterns, to forgive and move on with his life. Over the week, I began to feel an attraction towards him, wondering if it was because he was so open about his issues. The workshop had been intense, making us all feel raw with emotion. There were only six of us in our small group, and by the time it was over, we all agreed to stay in touch with each other as we went off to our own lives and careers. Jim left us with an open invitation to whomever wanted to visit London, his home was open to us. As a group we exchanged phone numbers and addresses. We all shared letters several times a year.

When I received my diagnosis, I wrote to Jim sharing the horrors of it all. A week or two later Jim called, giving me support and reassurance. He also offered Buzz and me, or friends or family, a place to stay if we should ever come to England. He encouraged me to come after chemotherapy saying, "Europe is only seven hours away. No big deal!" I put the whole idea on the back burner, but there was a glimmer of hope with Jim's offer. I decided to test the waters.

When I mentioned to Ann that after my chemotherapy was completed, I would like to take a trip to Europe, she quickly said, "No, I'm just too afraid to fly."

I was disappointed, but not surprised, as she had struggled with fear of flying for a long time. On the other hand, Laurie, who had been to Europe, raved about the architecture and beauty of the cities she visited. She was thrilled with the idea of going again and said a resounding, "Yes!"

In place of Ann, I asked my good friend, Maureen, who immediately responded, "Absolutely! You know I am always ready for an adventure! Besides, I am way overdue for a visit to see Diana and JF (her sister and brother-in-law residing in Belgium.) I'm sure we can stay with them in Brussels."

Buzz again declined when I asked him if he wanted to go with us, but the truth was, I wanted to go without him. We were not in a good place at that time. I really think we needed a break from each other, although neither of us said as much.

149

I kept him apprised of how we were going to stay with others, so spending money would not be an issue.

In those months prior to going to London, Buzz had been working six to seven days a week, striving to keep us financially stable. Each evening, we watched TV together. Around ten o'clock I would say, "It's getting late. I'm tired. Are you coming to bed?"

"I'm not tired. I will be up later," he would reply.

I went to sleep remembering his promise to come upstairs, and upon awakening in the middle of the night, I would reach out to touch him, but he was never there – my heart would sink with hurt and disappointment. I seldom saw him as he worked in the office all day and slept on the couch every night, falling asleep while watching TV. Some nights I went upstairs without saying good night, thinking, *I'll just ignore him the way he is ignoring me.* Other times, I told him how lonely, hurt and disconnected I felt sleeping alone. I was starved for intimacy and missed him. But it didn't seem to matter to him. I finally gave up, thinking there are worse things in a marriage. I was grateful to Buzz for shouldering the financial burden, however, as I was soon to discover, the hurt and disappointment in any relationship does not just magically disappear due to a geographical separation or a decision to give up. It lay deep within me.

Laurie bought my ticket with some of her flight miles. Between the three of us, with friends and family in Europe we planned our trip around staying with them, saving quite a bit of money. It looked like this trip could become a reality. I also felt the pressure and fear of the cancer returning and the desire to experience this trip while I had the time and was healthy.

The idea of going to Europe was a wonderful focus and when treatment was over, Laurie, Maureen and I would often talk and plan what we should bring and where we would visit. Treatment ended in late winter and I thought I would be strong enough to go in the fall around my birthday. Besides, by that time I was hoping I would have some hair growth.

My last CAT scan was clean and beautiful. I was still taking Zoloft for depression, HRT for menopause, and Xanax at night for sleep. Chinese herbs and nutritional supplements were helping my energy levels increase. I began bicycling every day to build my strength for the trip. This trip was also a celebration of my birthday. Getting older no longer had a negative impact. I was thrilled to be turning fifty!

Europe was an incredible piece of heaven exploring with Laurie and Maureen. I felt alive, bursting with excitement and anticipation – absorbed and present in every moment. Gratitude and joy-filled bliss were my constant companions. Traveling with women, talking, sharing 'women's talk,' completely free to plan each day and choose what picturesque place to become immersed in. In London, we ate out every night, toured the Tower of London, attended a stage production of *Sunset Boulevard* with Rita Moreno, shopped at Selfridges and explored St. Paul's Cathedral where Princess Diana was married. Our pace was slow – no rushing from one site to the next. Both Laurie and Maureen were sweetly considerate of my energy levels and timetable.

In Brussels, we stayed with Diana, Maureen's sister, in her lovely home in the country. It was here when I noticed how much better I felt being in the country. Nature surrounded me. It became as intimate as an embrace. We toured Ghent, and Bruges, the lace capital of the world, but it was the long walks in the beautiful Belgian countryside that made my heart explode with gratitude. Diana, her husband, JF, and their son, Ryan, drove us to Provence and we stayed in their quaint vacation home in Buisson, visiting beautiful places nearby, such as Vaison-la-Romaine, the Roman ruins, Brant, and Avignon, just to name a few.

Our next stop was Lyon, where we stayed with Bernard and Josette, the parents of one of Laurie and her husband, Terry's, foreign exchange students, who had spent a summer with them. Bernard took us to Aix les Bains near the Swiss Alps, driving past Mt. Blanc, which is the tallest mountain in Europe. I caught glimpses of the Nature of it all.

We called on the parents of another of Laurie and Terry's exchange students, Thoma, when we arrived in Paris. They owned a hotel there and were gracious enough to offer us accommodations. The highlight for me was eating at Le Procope, a restaurant that dates back to 1686. Voltaire and Victor Hugo often ate there as well as Ben Franklin. It is credited to be where the French Revolution was born.

Our pace was slow throughout the trip. Everywhere we went, we were wined and dined. I wrote in my journal:

Everyday has been a jewel. I have felt a total lack of stress. I feel a little guilty – I have written only one postcard home.

Although we stayed busy throughout the trip, there was a calmness settling inside of me. With deep introspection, I was mulling over my relationship with Buzz, and trying to re-evaluate how I wanted to live my life. When we got to London, Jim met us. Just seeing him, I felt the allure again. I questioned the sudden temptation. Passion – does passion and desire deserve acknowledgement? I don't know, but I have come to realize that it didn't need to be answered, it served its purpose. It brought me alive, my senses were restored. I again felt the power of being a woman. No, I did not share these feelings with Jim nor did he return or respond to my unspoken attraction, although he probably knew. Buzz and I had just been through so much dealing with the cancer.

Looking back, I can see even more clearly now how illness can sometimes wreak havoc within a marriage. It became obvious that we immediately went into survival mode as we each took a different path to cope with my diagnosis and treatment. As the sick spouse, and fueled by fear, I focused all my energy on healing. The desire to heal was the ultimate goal; sex and desire had little place during that time. When treatment was over, I wanted to get away from the memories of being ill. I yearned to feel like an attractive woman again, feeling the need to desire and be desired, all of those things that were stripped from me when I was sick.

At the same time, I now realize – although I had all along acknowledged how grateful I was for Buzz and his ability to keep everything together, but, because of my own self-absorption with cancer and healing, I don't think it really sunk in how deep the pain had gone for him, and how really hard his struggle was. Sure, there were financial issues, single parenting and such, but his own emotional center had been totally upended. He loved me and he was terrified and buried himself in other issues, just trying to make it through. It had been a rollercoaster ride of emotions for him. Now I could see more than ever that Buzz and I communicated well when we took the time; however, through our stress, we began to grow apart, silently, stoically, keeping our wounded thoughts to ourselves. Thank God for the quiet times in Europe. I needed this.

When I returned home, I felt this overwhelming guilt roll through me, as if I had committed some hideous sin. I wrote a letter to Jim, sharing the attraction I felt for him, and that it would be better if we ended our friendship. I thought by being honest and putting everything on the page, that my attraction would dissipate. I'm sure it took him by surprise, or maybe it didn't. Maybe he noticed, but was man enough not to respond. He was close to becoming engaged and had never said or done anything inappropriate. I kept a copy of the letter, read it a couple of times, then tore it into little pieces. I did not want anyone to read it. Then, I threw it in the wastebasket. Like a ritual, it was over and I knew it was time to focus on Buzz and our relationship.

Our bonds were much deeper than just a fling built up in my mind. I knew that being attracted to others is a part of human nature, but acting upon it is totally another thing, no matter the rejection and hurt I felt by Buzz's behavior. When I left for Europe, I was deeply committed to my husband and when I returned, I was even more so.

To my horror, Buzz found the torn copy of the letter and painstakingly taped it together, read it, placed it in an envelope and then slipped the envelope under the bedroom door. My heart sank as I opened the envelope and saw the taped, reconstructed letter. I could not imagine how he was able to put that letter together – the pieces were very, very small! I could only envision his painful determination to keep going and make sense of the letter. A part of me was relieved. I immediately went downstairs to find him.

"I'm sorry you found the letter and that I caused you pain."

His eyes flashed with hurt and anger. "After all I have sacrificed this past year, terrified of you dying and doing my best to keep us together financially and emotionally and now I have to deal with this?" His hand was shaking while pointing to the torn letter. "I love you, but I need time to work through this gut punch."

I nodded in agreement. "I will give you plenty of space." Then, I continued. "I'll admit that I was emotionally unfaithful to you in my attraction to Jim, and dishonest about my feelings." I added, "Truthfully, another part of me feels a little 'satisfied' to see you hurting the way you have hurt me in the past." He nodded as if he understood and walked away. We both needed time to gather our thoughts and do some soul searching before we spoke again.

I wondered about the power of such an attraction and why it had swept over me again. In London, I felt pretty for the first time in months, excited and thrilled to be alive. It didn't help when I shared this attraction for Jim with friends in London who said, "You have been to hell and back – Go ahead, fuck your brains out!"

I was shocked by their response, but in truth, I did think about it. But sex was not the answer. Somewhere deep inside of me, I feel as if I have used Jim to show me the light. Through all of this, incredibly, I have felt loved by God. I was sad I had hurt Buzz, yet there was a knowing, that as a couple, this was the 'healing fire' we needed.

At the time I wrote in my journal about this attraction to Jim, I had forgotten that Jim and I had no hurtful history together. We shared a similar father-abandonment wound. This certainly was my childhood hurt from my workaholic German parents, who received the same hurt from their own parents. A generational pattern passed down from parent to parent.

This was not just about some illicit sexual fix to satisfy a passing sexual desire. From my core, I wanted to *live*, with a passionate desire to *be* in this world as an authentic human being, trusting that God would take me where I needed to go professionally and personally. Embracing every moment whether happy or hurtful, open to the awe and wonder of life was my deepest gut-wrenching desire. The whole experience of Europe became the birthing ground that opened me to the fact that I could never go back to my shallow, ignorant world before cancer, blind to the sacred, simple, symmetry in the ordinary rhythm of life.

Being married for over twenty-five years, Buzz and I assumed we knew what the other needed and now we learned, that even when we ask each other we may not know what we need! In the aftermath of treatment, we became complacent in recognizing the gifts and talents each other brought to the marriage. Truthfully, this began two years before the cancer diagnosis. I spent a grueling two years completing my master's degree, still working in my wallpapering and painting business, taking care of the house and parenting. Being self-employed as a builder/remodeler, Buzz's energy was focused on the endless details of completing a project and finding another one. So much pressure to survive and pay the bills! And then cancer.

Our marriage was never 'easy street,' each of us bringing our own baggage. However, from the beginning we knew our relationship would never survive on the 'gooey-love' feeling alone without making a commitment and a decision to love one another. Throughout our marriage there was more positive about our relationship than negative and what tipped the scales in our favor was a shared spirituality, humor, seeking help when we needed it and a very important 'wow-factor' – he can dance!

Little by little, each in our own way, we made a stronger effort to spend time together and to communicate in a more honest, assertive, and respectful manner. Making the decision to see a marriage counselor really helped us see the difference in how we each coped with stress, which brought our understanding to a new level. We looked for ways to strengthen our marriage, such as, taking turns planning special date nights, setting aside time each morning to have coffee or tea together and talk about the day, taking more dance lessons, and joining a Cotillion Club where we could 'dress up' and dance to a live orchestra five times a year. Also, we became more sensitive to the power of non-sexual 'touch' for connection – holding hands, massaging feet and heads, and hugging. As children, neither one of us received enough affirmation from our fathers, and so as adults, were more inclined to comment on the negative than the positive. Therefore, we made a conscious effort to express our appreciation for each other.

To this day, we can fall into a pattern of putting work first over nurturing our relationship. However, we are getting very good at recognizing this tendency and can say, 'Stop!'

It was fortunate we took the time and energy to shore up our relationship. We didn't know it fully then, but a dark cloud was beginning to appear on the horizon, one that envelops many cancer survivors and leaves destroyed marriages in its wake.

Chapter 11 – Bankruptcy

"To the Cherokee worry is the dalala, the woodpecker, pecking away on the roof…but how do we handle this woodpecker called worry? By seeing it for what it is – a bird that causes damage."
~Joyce Sequichie Hifler

We were in a financial crisis. Whatever small savings we had before the cancer was now gone. Most of the alternative therapies were not covered by insurance, so we charged them.

Buzz did not have much work during what should have been a busy time of year. My friends, Anxious and Afraid, the ones that showed up on the day I was diagnosed with cancer, were back keeping me company every night with their constant chatter. They were relentless – *You will lose your home. Shame on you for not being able to make it financially. All of your friends will retire soon. You need to go back to work. Who do you think you are taking all this time off?* Every day, I battled with myself about not working.

At my core, I am not a gut person, one who reacts to life with an immediate spontaneous, intuitive response. I am a head person – my control tower is the brain. I have always been one who steps back and analyzes the situation and proceeds in an orderly fashion. However, my gut was speaking loud and clear. I knew I needed to be home, focused on helping Buzz in the office and being home for my daughters. My gut told me that if I went back to work full time, the cancer would come back. Working forty hours a week, with two young daughters still at home, and caring for two acres of property would consume me – taking all my energy. I needed more time to heal – to build up my energy reserves – to become stronger in body, mind and spirit.

We borrowed money from Terry, my brother-in-law, while I also had a garage sale and was able to pay a few overdue bills. One day, when I had $20 in my checking account and the credit card companies started to call, I made a shocking discovery. The possibility of personal bankruptcy was similar to the diagnosis of a terminal lymphoma. I asked myself how was personal bankruptcy different from facing death and dealing with cancer? The answer came quickly. There was no shame in being diagnosed with cancer. Being 'diagnosed' with bankruptcy, as the only option back to solvency, was loaded with societal shame. For years, not only have I secretly carried the emotional baggage of feeling as if I wasn't good enough, now all the world will know I/we do not measure up to what society considers 'successful.' I will have a huge 'B' tattooed across my forehead.

The possibility of personal bankruptcy turned into a reality. After meeting with a financial advisor, we were counseled to file for Chapter 13, a personal bankruptcy not business bankruptcy. The court date rapidly appeared and we found ourselves in a crowded courtroom with other bankruptcy applicants. I hurriedly scanned the room, praying that no one would recognize us. When I did not see anyone I knew, I breathed a sigh of relief. Our name came up quickly and the judge told us that we must pay $500 a month for five years and that the payments *must* be on time. The money will be doled out to all our creditors through the court system. I shared this shameful secret with few people, praying that no one would read the lists of bankruptcies in the newspaper.

The next morning, sipping my herbal tea, I started to reflect on my bruised bankruptcy ego. In a flash, a shame spiral wrapped itself around me, creating an abyss of negative thoughts. Just as quickly, some surprising thoughts came floating down my stream of consciousness – *'Be quiet.'* *You know, you are really brave. Think about the courage it took for you to say 'no' about going back to work to fix this money problem. Especially since, 'What will the neighbors think' is such a deeply engrained message in you. You chose healing over ego.'*

The golden truth that I learned through this painful, ego-crushing experience was that bankruptcy did not have the power to name who I was. I did not allow the shame of bankruptcy to deter me from my focus on healing. Now that my body was recovering from treatment and there was no more evidence of the cancer, I had a deeper resolve to center on my mind, becoming more conscious and mindful of my thoughts, feelings, and motivations. I asked God every day, "What lesson are you teaching me today in this never-ending 'earth school?'"

Chapter 12 – More Synchronicity

"Storms in life can bring healing, wholeness and holiness. Choose life over fear of living. Life will bring more life."
~Matthew Linn, S.J.

Over the next three years, I immersed myself in healing: eating nutritiously, exercising, attending spiritual retreats, strengthening my Centering Prayer practice, reading spiritual books and journaling. Now, I was feeling a gentle readiness to return to my work of psychotherapy. Excited about resuming work, I became a little fearful. The voices of Fear and Trepidation crept in, voicing their concerns about my competence to heal others. One day while sitting in silence, after Centering Prayer, I heard the words – *In my name you will hold my lambs.* A powerful sense of relief poured over me. *Healing* was God's job and *holding* future clients with love and positive regard would be my job.

To further emphasize this message, several weeks later, out of the blue, I received a package in the mail from Josette, a friend we stayed with in Lyon, France, while we were touring Europe. She knew about my having cancer, but knew nothing about what God had said to me during my prayer time. I carefully opened the package that had *Fragile* written all over it. Slowly peeling away the bubble wrap, I gasped at what I saw. I held in my hand a small statue of a shepherdess intricately painted, holding a lamb under one arm and a skein of wool in the other. Inside the box there was an explanation. She had sent me a 'santon,' a terra cotta figurine beautifully painted to place in a crèche scene. The figurines are very popular in France and could be any animal or person that might have been a part of the nativity scene. The lamb and the skein of wool were the shepherdess' gifts to the infant Jesus.

Feeling loved and affirmed, I patiently waited for the right time to return to work, knowing God would direct me. Soon after receiving the *santon,* a therapist friend of mine asked me to lunch. In the course of the conversation, as I shared my thoughts about returning to work, she suggested I call a local nonprofit agency, called Kairos Family Center, to see if they had any openings. During the initial phone interview, I had asked Jim, the senior therapist, what '*Kairos*' meant. He said, "*Kairos* is a Greek word and means *God's time* or *now is the time.*" He went on to explain, "Reverend Bill Clark, who started the agency, wanted a place where people could receive help and not have to wait a long time." Even before the face-to-face interview, I knew that 'Kairos' was where I would receive the love, support, and professional guidance I needed to complete my clinical hours.

For the next several years, I was caught up in my work at Kairos. I was happy, focused and inspired, and felt privileged to witness the courage, growth, and grace of the people who came for help. I continued to meditate every morning, exercised, took my herbs and supplementary vitamins, drank green tea, and ate more nutritiously.

I realized *fear* was lifting from my life and being replaced with *confidence.* I was unsure what to do with these new confident feelings, and at times I found myself slipping back into the old thinking of *I'm not good enough. I don't measure up. What of value do I have to offer?* With lightning speed, I could quickly become enmeshed in fear and forget my recent life lessons. I began to realize how entrenched this was in my life – to was as if I was not comfortable without some amount of fear operating! Soon after this revelation, I attended a lecture during Lent that continued the lesson I needed to learn about the power of fear.

The speaker, Father David Engbarth said: *"We are an angry people who have lost our souls. We live in an addicted society. We are addicted to 'things.' All addictions keep us afraid and out of touch with ourselves. Our addictions keep us from God, as we feel worthless, a nobody. We are too busy to challenge this addictive system."*

So, I asked myself, *What is my addiction?* Immediately, I knew the answer. I am addicted to Fear, Worry, and Perfection, which rob me of energy and put pressure on my loved ones. With this realization, I wanted to look deeper at the Fear that robbed me of the precious energy I needed to stay balanced and healed.

Soon after this revelation, I was meditating, and being unusually bombarded with negative, fearful thoughts. Frustrated and angry, I wondered where these fearful thoughts were coming from? Suddenly it occurred to me that the intensity of the emotions reminded me of a child's reaction to a frightening experience. Therefore, I knew that my initial response came from a terrified inner child. But what was most disturbing to me was to realize, for most of my adult life, this six-year old child has been 'driving the bus,' with the other parts of me taking a back seat, including the adult me.

This was an, aha moment. Before cancer, I read about and worked on inner-child issues. I knew I was not loved perfectly, and as a consequence, I formed beliefs about myself that disempowered me, such as, *I'm not good enough. I won't measure up. The world is a scary place. Money will keep me safe and happy.* I knew Fear was my middle name. I did not know Fear was six years old and in control of my life. Recognizing her, listening to her, understanding her role of trying to take care of me and to keep me from danger, I could finally accept and appreciate that part of me. This was a monumental step in my emotional healing. I was becoming a compassionate, forgiving observer of myself.

Learning to live in the present moment was the greatest lesson cancer taught me. All we have is this moment. Centering Prayer has helped me stay in the present. However, I recognized I needed more help to make 'living in the now' last longer than several minutes at a time! Frustrated about my perceived lack of progress, I turned to James Finley, a former Trappist monk mentored by Thomas Merton. Finley has written several books on spirituality and works as a clinical psychologist. His words put me back on the right path.

He wrote, "We find ourselves doing what we don't want to do, therefore, to stop the behavior we must find the tap root, the source, for the tap root causes blindness which leads to fear, which leads to clinging, which leads to suffering." He affirmed what I knew to be true: that a meditation practice helps us find the taproot, because to look deeply we need to become quiet and to slow down. Now, I was looking for perfection in my meditation practice. Finley said, "We need to *bow* and give ourselves up, surrender ourselves to God *just as we are*."

More pearls of wisdom from Jim Finley have kept me on the surrender path:

- Use the breath to slow down – focus on the in breath and the out breath.
- In meditation practice, one recognizes fairly quickly the inability to be present to God, as one instantly can be bombarded with thoughts and 'monkey mind' takes over.

- One can despair and give up, or, decide to go deeper and love yourself in your powerlessness and helplessness.

I discovered that as a result of spending twenty minutes a day in Centering Prayer, I slowly became more conscious and compassionately mindful of myself and others, more aware of the goodness and grace in life, and more aware of God's presence in everything. I became more mindful of the seeds of anger, envy, and fear that arose during the day, and prayed for them to be transformed. Thich Nhat Hanh, the Buddhist monk, asks, "Why water the seeds of your own unhappiness?"

I try not to judge my meditation practice anymore, even when 'monkey mind' envelops the entire twenty minutes. As gently as possible, I return to my breathing or sacred word and continue the practice. I know that the power and grace of the practice lie in my intention to connect with God, as I consent every day to be in the presence of God in those twenty minutes.

As I continued with my healing journey, reading, praying, journaling, seeking, and sharing, I continued to be surprised and pleased to see I was finding acceptance and compassion toward my own frailties as a human being. I was beginning to find, as Finley said, "comfort in my discomfort." What freedom to step out of the mind games of striving for perfection and accept all of my humanity – that as a human being, the chaff will always accompany the wheat.

Chapter 13 – Called to Stillness

"The journey that ultimately matters is deep into the stillness of oneself.
To go there is to be at home. To fail to travel there is to be forever
restless. It is there where one's life and spirit are united. In the silence,
the Word leaps down and is heard."
~N. Gordon Cosby

I'm drawn again to the comfortable chair by the window in my bedroom that overlooks a small wooded area on our property. Looking through the old mullioned windowpanes, I am intimately connected to this view. To the left, I can see a large section of the woods with paths that twist and turn, and to my right, there is part of the grassy backyard with a raised vegetable and flower-picking garden. As I look straight ahead, I see the Korean Sun Pear tree I planted as a birthday present to myself. A little further beyond, I see a special garden that is one of the entrances to the woods.

When I created this garden, my mother was ninety-five years old. Every Friday, I spent the day with her, always sharing my latest gardening project. When I expressed my interest in creating a garden that contained a majority of flowering bushes with a small flowering tree in the middle, Mom said she wanted to help me financially to make this garden a reality. As I thought about her love of flowers and Nature, I decided to name this garden in her honor. All my life, Mom, as my caretaker, taught me to see beauty with a sense of wonder. Inspired by her, I wanted this garden to honor all caretakers, men and women. I called it *Corinne's Corner*. As I gaze out the window, a little past Corinne's Corner, I see the old railroad bed and what is left of a rusty old gate used years ago to herd cows across the tracks for better grazing.

Through this window I have carefully observed seasons coming and going, the play of light on the trees, especially the golden maple outside my window marking another entrance to the woods, the many shades of color on the foliage as the seasons change, the animals occasionally coming into view, and how the weather plays with the landscape. I practice Centering Prayer at this window every day. It has become a sacred space to me. Its energy draws me in, not for the beauty of the space or the special objects I have placed on the windowsill, but for its sacredness as it holds my intention to consent to God's presence and action in that small space.

One day, during Centering Prayer, I heard the words – *Use the woods.* As with any thought that comes into my conscious mind during Centering Prayer, I gently let it go. Later, I reflected on those words. *What could they mean?* In the past several months, I felt God nudging me to share my spiritual journey and gardens with others. *But what would the woods have to do with that?* In the twenty-five years we had lived here, the small wooded area had only been used by our sons for dirt biking.

Later I confided to my women's prayer group that God was speaking to me about sharing my spiritual journey. Cathy, who is a former nun, and now married with three grown children, said she also felt God speaking to her about some form of ministry. Another woman said, "Why don't you do something together?"

After prayer and discussion over the next several weeks, Cathy and I decided to develop one-day retreats for women. The ideas and themes tumbled out of us: Awakening to the Divine; Return of the Mother; Bearing Fruit; Embracing the Shadow; Our Senses: Thresholds to the Soul; Forgiveness; and others. As we considered all these different themes for the day, I was certain of one aspect that was most important to me and had to become the umbrella theme of each retreat, and that was Silence. Cancer and the debilitating toxic chemotherapy had forced me to slow down and learn the value of silence.

Having decided to join with Cathy in developing day retreats using Nature as our teacher, I was certain we needed to include the small wooded area along with the yard surrounding my home. I was reminded of the hero's journey in every fairy tale and there was often a 'woods experience' where the hero/heroine becomes lost in the woods and has to overcome fear and hardship to find their way home. Since we are all called to the hero's journey, with those words, *'Use the woods,'* I sensed that God wanted me to clear out the scrub brush and buckthorn in the woods, making it possible for people to walk the woods as a metaphor for their own 'woods experience.'

The wooded area around our home constitutes about a third of an acre. Walking in the woods, I began to envision where paths could be placed. But how would I make the paths? I had heard that the township would drop off bark chips for free. Excited, about this prospect, I called and made arrangements to have the chips dropped off.

On a very hot and humid day, with a strong breeze blowing, the freshly ground chips from felled trees were delivered. Slathered down with mosquito repellant, I attached a cart to the old rusty tractor/lawn mower and maneuvered the cart with great difficulty close to the bark chip pile. I asked Mindy, our youngest, to help me begin this daunting task of creating paths.

"Mom, what are we doing?" she asked, as she eyed the massive pile of chips about as tall as her.

In a rather forced, chirpy voice, trying to sound positive so as to engage her in this project I said, "We are going to make paths in the woods!"

She rolled her eyes and asked, "Why?" as if I had suggested the nuttiest thing she had ever heard in her ten years on the planet.

With an upbeat voice I said, "Do you remember all the fairy tales I read to you and movies you have seen about people who have been lost in the woods – like Hansel and Gretel, Beauty and the Beast, Snow White?"

She nodded and I continued.

"At first, they were so scared and didn't know which way to go, but they all made it out of the woods, after having learned wonderful lessons about how smart and strong they really were. I want people to experience that in these woods – they are loved by God, and God will help them through any difficulty – like God helped me through cancer."

In retrospect, it was a rather long-winded explanation, but Mindy shrugged her shoulders and began to shovel bark chips into the cart. Later, when Buzz asked what she did all day, very matter-of-factly she said, "I helped Mom with her God Paths."

I laughed.

At one point or another, all my children helped with the God Paths.

Soon, Cathy and I started to host and lead day retreats with the umbrella theme of "Called to Stillness," with different underlying themes.

Our mission statement for the retreats became:

'To provide a safe place to experience the Sacred. We welcome all, honoring each person's journey of faith. Our hope is through Nature, journaling, sharing,

music, meditation, and group prayer that each person may experience the Divine within themselves and others.'

During the retreats, it was Cathy's and my experience that when we came together as a group with our spirits yielding to the healing grace of God, we became awakened to God, who St. Catherine of Siena called, the 'Mad Lover,' a God who has fallen madly in love with his creatures and creation.

Mary, a middle-aged woman with grown children, and a soon-to-be grandmother, attended the first retreat. She had just been diagnosed with breast cancer. After spending some quiet time in Nature reflecting on God's love, Mary shared with the group, "I found myself in the woods and saw a huge log, so I sat down. Growing next to the log was an enormous plant with huge leaves that looked like angel wings. Unexpectedly, I felt protected, calm and safe, that no matter what treatment lay ahead of me – a strong sense that all is well came over me."

What Mary did not know is that the plant she sat next to is called *broadleaf*, a weed with burrs that multiplies easily with deep roots. On the 'to do' list for my preparation for the retreat was to dig out as many of the broadleaf weeds in the woods as I could, but fortunately I did not have the time! The wisdom of Ralph Waldo Emerson came to mind: "Weed – a plant whose virtues have not yet been discovered."

After the first retreat, there was never a question of *Will God really speak to whoever attends?* The question became, *How? How will God manifest love this time?*

At another retreat, Martha, a middle-aged woman, who was recently divorced, wrote a prayer to God. She said:

Dear God,
I look in wonder at your creation. I see and feel your
presence everywhere. In my Nature walk I came to a
fork in the woods, two ways to go. Which way, God? I
realize I have always had a choice about what path to
take and, I have always had a choice of how I will
respond to life.
Every choice I made was the right one because I
learned lessons that helped me become who I am. My
heart is full.

It became apparent to me that we need two important qualities on our healing journey: openness and a sense of adventure. A spiritual journey also consists of the awareness of the Divine Presence in all things and taking the energy of that loving awareness into all of creation. Along with the exploration into the depths of my shadow, my ability to *see* expanded. I often saw life with the freshness of a child, with wonder and openness.

One winter day, I awoke to a cold and bright sunny day. It was four degrees outside. Wrapped in a warm blanket, I sat mesmerized by the window. Looking like soft sparkling angel wings, the condensation on the old storm windows covered the entire window, except for a small portion at the top. Shining through the crystal condensation, the sun was almost blinding. Dazzling designs of the ice crystals danced before me, magical and fairy-like in their brilliance and uniqueness. Through the tiny clear opening at the top of the window, I felt the warmth of the sun and saw bare tree branches silhouetted against the blue sky. Rare beauty to behold – a gift from the season of winter.

Later in the day, I stopped for a moment watching the squirrels romp and play in the leafless trees. Perfectly balanced, they jumped from one branch to another. Always looking for a way around the birdseed baffles, they followed a 'squirrel highway' outside my window to the food source. I wondered, how do they know what thin branch will hold their weight as they leap crisscrossing from branch to branch? Quick, nimble and  surefooted are these playful, tenacious animals. Lessons from the squirrels: never give up, trust your instincts, play is elemental to living, stay grounded to the earth while balancing the needs of your body, mind and spirit.

The next afternoon, on a cold, sunny December day, I decided to continue my meditation practice by taking a walk. The air smelled crisp and clean. Several days earlier we had received the first heavy snowfall. The branches of the trees were still heavy with snow and the sun accentuated the dazzling beauty of the snow crystals draping the tree branches. I headed toward the old railroad bed south of the house, which was now a bike path. The bark chip path emitted a new sound as the ground under the heavy spread of chips had partially frozen and heaved the bark chips upward. My feet sank into the heavy mixture of snow and decaying matter with a lovely crunch. Wafting upward, I could smell the musky, organic scent of the earth.

Walking along the railroad bed, I pondered the number of times the trains had passed by on this bed since the Minnesota and Northwestern Railroad Company had purchased the rights to lay tracks in 1886. I imagined myself riding on one of those trains and God told me to get off here to become a temporary guardian of this land. *"Thank you God for the honor of caring for this small piece of earth,"* I whispered.

As I came to the end of the property on the old rail bed, I slid down the embankment and walked into the woods. Looking at the old Black Locust trees, I wondered at all they had seen over the years. I sat on a nearby bench with the sun warming my face. My eyes rested on a black locust tree that we had trimmed in the fall. It was over a hundred years old still standing straight and tall. Without thinking, I rose and walked over to the tree and wrapped my arms around it. Pressing my cheek against the rough bark I could sense the essence of God in this tree – the strength, the energy and eternal groundedness.

The tree, God and I were one.

Experiencing Nature in these sacramental moments, I knew I was on holy ground in the divinity of what just is. It is in the ordinary that God embraces and sustains us. I was learning how to *be* so I could experience God in these ordinary, yet extraordinary happenings.

I recognized how much I loved the days of winter especially the starkness of the trees, naked, completely exposed. I could see the beautiful limbs silhouetted against the early evening sky, and all the animals and birds that rest and play in the branches. In winter, nothing is hidden; all is exposed, just as I am exposed when entering into the darkness and winter of my soul. If I look under the dead leaves and bark, I will find strong, fresh growth waiting for the light  of recognition and love, so I can grow and flourish.

Albert Camus says, "In the midst of winter, I finally learned that there was in me an invincible summer."

In the near distant future, this awareness would be sorely tested.

Chapter 14 – The Journey Continues:

"We wait in the darkness!
Come, all ye who listen,
Help in our night journey:
Now no sun is shining;
Now no star is glowing;
Come show us the pathway:
The night is not friendly:
The moon has forgot[ten] us,
We wait in the darkness!"
~Iroquois Prayer

Five years passed since the diagnosis of Non-Hodgkin's lymphoma. I happily returned to my chosen profession as a psychotherapist. Back at work for two years, getting very close to completing my clinical hours to take the state boards, my life dramatically changed again.

One cold day in late fall after taking a warm soaking bath; I began the ritual of rubbing lotion over my body. My heart began to pound as I felt something different in my left breast. *What is this? Could it be a lump? Dear God, no!*

I carefully, and very slowly checked my left breast again and then, for a sense of comparison, I checked my right breast. They felt different. I could barely breathe.

How could this be? I had a breast checkup only a month ago.

I hastily dressed and stumbled down the stairs in a panic looking for a phone book. I wanted someone to help me figure this out *now*. Shaking, I ran to the phone and leafed through the yellow pages looking for a breast specialist in the area, any breast specialist. I didn't care. I was desperate for information. With my voice trembling I called and explained my concern to the receptionist who was able to schedule an appointment the next day. Hanging up the phone, I calmed down a little. *After all, what does a cancerous lump in the breast feel like? Perhaps, it was fatty tissue or a cyst.*

After the Asian doctor examined my breast, with a compassionate, concerned look on his face he confirmed my worse fear and said, "Yes, this is a suspicious lump and you were right in coming to see me. We will need to schedule a biopsy."

I immediately thought this was the lymphoma returning. I was on a roller-coaster ride of emotions, which was very familiar territory for me. The surgeon assured me the results would be in on that following Monday.

While waiting for the results, I decided to attend a weekend retreat I had scheduled over a year ago at the Cenacle. The original weekend presenter cancelled. He was fearful of flying after 9/11, even though it was several months after the attack. I wasn't even certain of the new presenter's topic, but I didn't care. I felt compelled to attend, as if there was something waiting for me, or something I needed to know. Other than my husband, very few family members knew about the biopsy. I did not want to raise undo alarm and concern.

The weekend turned out to be an unexpected blessing, as the retreat focused on the poem, *The Living Flame of Love* by St. John of the Cross, presented by Sister Mary Meegan. Throughout the weekend, Sister Mary analyzed each stanza of the poem, providing an explanation of what St. John meant when he wrote the poem centuries earlier, around 1584. I do not remember exactly what Sister Mary said, but somehow the essence of the poem entered my spirit, and I memorized and clung to the words.

In the poem, St. John talks about sacramental moments on earth in which God communicates with a special closeness to us. In those moments, we are awake and aware of this sacred union. St. John uses symbols to describe some of these intense encounters like: living flames, delightful wounds, lamps of fire, exquisite light, warmth, and sweet breathing. Reading the poem over and over, especially the last stanza;

> *"And in your sweet breathing,*
> *Filled with good and glory,*
> *How tenderly you swell my heart with love."*

I experienced God holding me. It was as if we were as close as my breath. This closeness made the waiting to see if the cancer had returned bearable. For the most part over the weekend, I stayed in the present moment – a miracle for me, given my tendency to cave into fearful scenarios of 'what if's.'

On Sunday evening, I was home with Buzz who greeted me warmly with a lovely dinner he had prepared. My sister, Laurie, joined us, as she wanted to know if I had heard anything about the biopsy results. After eating, the children went upstairs to do their homework and Buzz, Laurie and I sat relaxed in the family room as I shared about the retreat weekend still bathed in the sweetness of the experience. My friend Sharon from graduate school unexpectedly stopped by and I calmly shared the news with her that we were waiting for the results of a breast biopsy. The phone suddenly rang and Buzz told me that the surgeon who did the biopsy wished to speak to me.

"I'm sorry to bother you on a Sunday evening, but I know you are anxious to hear the results," the doctor said. He paused and then continued, "The medical test results confirm that you have breast cancer. I'm very sorry."

What is it about receiving potentially threatening news that turns spiritual resolve into jelly?

When I heard the doctor's words, the sweetness of the weekend retreat quickly melted away and shifted to shock, fear and outrage. A devout Christian, Sharon began to lead us all in prayer, but all I wanted to do was to scream *Fuck* at God. I was sobbing, while everyone else was praying and asking for divine intervention. I wanted divine intervention, too, but all I could think of was – *What are you fucking thinking, God?*

A local breast surgeon had done the biopsy, but I knew I wanted to return to Northwestern, back to the doctors that helped me through non-Hodgkin's lymphoma. I was informed that I would need a breast surgeon to remove the cancer from my breast, and to see if the cancer had spread, a plastic surgeon to repair my breast and make it match the other breast, whether I have a mastectomy or lumpectomy. I would also need an oncologist to handle chemotherapy.

Several weeks later, meeting with the cancer team at Northwestern, I was given my options. The breast surgeon, while looking at me, calmly began to speak, "We suspect you have breast cancer with nodal involvement. If you want a lumpectomy, we need to remove a quadrant of your breast, and, at the same time, test the nodes on your left side under your armpit to see if the cancer has spread. We will remove your breast if you like – or if you choose a lumpectomy, you can have plastic surgery by taking a part of your back muscle to fill in the hole where the cancer was removed."

I was overwhelmed. Once again, Laurie, my rock, with her calm, scientific, logical, mind told me, "We will proceed one step at a time. There is a somewhat standard treatment for breast cancer. We just need to wait for more information."

As if reading my mind, the doctor added, "And by the way, this cancer has nothing to do with non-Hodgkin's lymphoma."

I do know I was warned at the beginning of chemotherapy for non-Hodgkin's lymphoma, that although chemotherapy could save my life, a possible side effect of the toxic drugs could predispose me to lung cancer and leukemia. There was no mention of breast cancer. However, around the time of the breast cancer diagnosis a clinical study was reported all over the news. This study revealed the dangers of taking Hormone Replacement Therapy (HRT) to help women through menopause. A long-term research study warned women who took HRT that the chance of getting breast cancer was significantly increased. I was into my fourth year of taking those drugs and sorrowfully regretted my decision. I was left pondering the question – Was *it the non-Hodgkin's lymphoma chemotherapy that caused the breast cancer? Or the HRT? Or dumb luck.* No one seemed to know.

My sister and I left the office and I returned home, facing the next few weeks as though the peace from the weekend retreat never happened.

Several days after I met with the oncology team, I experienced a vivid, terrifying dream. It shook my entire being. Waking up with my heart pounding, I slowly rolled over picking up my pen to write down the dream before it could vanish from memory. I called it Asian Man Dream.

I felt it held life or death information for me, but I knew I could not explore this dream just as I was preparing for breast surgery. I decided then, that when the time was right, I would go see Barbara, a psychotherapist who works with dreams. I wanted her help working through my grief, disappointment, anger and fear – and to explore the deeper levels of this terrifying dream. But that had to wait, along with just about everything else. I needed to take a breath and calm down.

I found myself in a dark place.

There was no light.

I was so close to beginning a private counseling practice, the culmination of years of schooling and clinical practice doing what I love – helping others to integrate body, mind and spirit. My whole being railed at God as I grappled with anger, fear, and anxiety about the future.

Why God? Where am I now? When I know you have divinely directed me into this healing profession.

When I have finally arrived at a place doing what I love, feeling completely alive. What do you fucking want from me?

Lymphoma is not enough? What do I need to learn this time? Isn't it someone else's turn?

I live my life wondering about lymphoma returning and now I have to worry about breast cancer, too! What are you thinking, God?

Why this?

Why now?

As the days passed, I slowly began to think of God's acts of faithfulness in the lives of people I knew. Certainly, I was not the only person to suffer from sorrow and disappointment.

I thought of my niece, Jenny, a young woman with two small children who became a paraplegic after a tragic car accident on her way to work. With grace and dignity, she accepted her fate and saw the blessings that came from her disability. I remembered clients of mine who had come from abusive childhoods and found the strength to harness that negative energy turning it into an unbelievably positive force of present moment empowerment.

Other clients had left marriages that were no longer life-giving and had transformed their grief and broken dreams into a new life. Older clients cared for sick parents or spouses, or had taken in their children's children, sacrificing their dreams to care for another. They all faced the future with dignity and grace, stepping out into the unknown, and had found that God was there.

My memories became a turning point and virgin hope stirred quietly in the dark recesses of my bruised, betrayed heart. Another significant memory came to light.

One day as I was struggling with this new cancer diagnosis, I picked up an old journal and began reading an entry about the day my youngest daughter, Mindy was diagnosed with juvenile diabetes. She was only six when this was discovered and she had been immediately put into the hospital for a week and introduced to the world of shots and pinpricks multiple times a day. I watched as her sweet innocence was destroyed: *The world was not a safe place anymore.* In my arms, and sobbing she would ask me over and over, "Why is this happening, Mom?"

Watching his little sister, her brother Nick only fifteen at the time, kept saying, "Why couldn't this have happened to me? Why her? She is so little."

I was in my early forties at the time, four years before the first diagnosis of cancer, and up to that point in my life, had felt protected by God – feeling that horrible things only happened to other people. With her diagnosis, I felt betrayed and abandoned by God. I didn't speak to God or actively seek a spiritual connection for two years.

Buzz could see I was struggling and asked if we could attend a retreat at the Cenacle. I agreed to attend because my husband wanted to go, and I knew I needed help working through the process of forgiving God for Mindy's diagnosis.

Father Matt Linn, a Jesuit priest, led the weekend retreat on *Forgiveness.*

The talks throughout the weekend were interesting, giving me food for thought, but my heart was still unforgiving and hard toward God. Before Sunday morning Mass, which was open to the public as well as the retreatants, Father Linn addressed the congregation.

"Would everyone please exchange one shoe with someone else and wear that shoe the entire Mass? You will have one of your own shoes and one of your neighbor's." He went on to explain, "We cannot possibly forgive one another, unless we understand where that person is coming from. We must for a while "walk in their shoes."

Everyone looked around a little apprehensively, and timidly began to exchange shoes. I thought, *I will exchange one of my shoes for one of Buzz's – that will be easier.* I slipped off my shoe and looked up. Father Linn had left the altar and was walking toward me holding out his shoe. I took his rather large, wide, worn brown leather sandal, and gave him my size 7 flat. He carried my shoe back to the altar, leaned down and slipped on my flat of which he could barely fit his toes. He shuffled along in my shoe the whole time he celebrated Mass. To me, it was as if Jesus was wearing my shoe, and deeply connected to my betrayal, as I was trying to be connected to the hurts in Father Linn's life.

There was a modern metal cross hanging behind the altar with the crucified Christ. During the Mass, as I was standing looking at the cross, I remembered that Jesus had also cried out to God asking, "My God, my God, why have you forsaken me?" Very much like in the poem of St. John of the Cross, a warm, bright Presence filled my heart. With tears rolling down my cheeks, I realized I was in good company. I was not the only one who had felt betrayed and abandoned by

God. The church was filled with people – why did Father Linn choose me? Life is full of *mystery* – and *awe* – and always, *amazing grace.*

In that moment, of reading the past journal entry I realized that all is well, that God understands, supports and deeply loves us in our humanity. However, it is true – God protects us from nothing, yet sustains us in everything. I wondered how I could have forgotten this profound God moment?

And so, I began to notice the Presence in small things: in a flower that I grew from a bulb, in the playful dance of squirrels as they chased each other, in the glorious pink and purple sunsets of winter, in the beauty of a snowy day watching my loved ones playfully shovel snow.

Nature had always helped to heal my soul, and the more time I spent in my gardens, the more I felt the Presence I so longed for. I realized that as I stayed in the present moment with the beauty of Nature, there were periods of time when thoughts of cancer were expelled from my mind. *I don't know why I have cancer again,* I thought to myself, *I have given up the whys and choose to trust this Presence, living in the mystery dancing in the dark. After all, as Clarissa Pinkola Estes says, "Dancing is the soul's greatest joy."*

Chapter 15 – Dancing in the Dark

"Darkness, the absence of light. Not being able to see – either having to grope my way to a familiar destination, to having to crawl cautiously to an unfamiliar place, testing the ground each step of the way. What perils lie in my path? Where am I? What inner light can guide me when I am lost and cannot see at all?"
~Elaine Emeth

How does one actually dance in the dark? Days after my firm resolution to trust God and 'dance' my life, I found myself sinking into the quagmire of questions about treatment and decisions. Despondent, I wondered, how would I ever get through treatment for another cancer?

After much deliberation, I decided to have a quadrant lumpectomy. The research showed that cancer could come back just as easily in the chest wall if I had a mastectomy versus a lumpectomy. The surgeons explained that when the breast surgeon was finished checking the sentinel node in my armpit to see if the cancer had spread to other nodes, and had removed the cancer tumor from my breast, and was certain the margins were clear of cancer, the plastic surgeon would take over. He would remove a portion of my back muscle and tuck it through the opening in my armpit where the nodes were tested; and then place the back muscle in my left breast to fill in where the breast tissue was removed. This was called an 'endoscopic latissimus flap,' a relatively new procedure that had been done only fifteen times by this surgeon who developed the method. Having the breast repaired at the same time as the tumor was removed meant that I only required major surgery once.

Several weeks after the biopsy, very early in the morning, Buzz, Laurie and I headed out to Northwestern

Memorial Hospital in Chicago. It seemed strange to sail into the city with very little traffic. Laurie and Buzz made light conversation as they could sense my somber, fearful mood. Buzz dropped us off in front of the hospital, so he could park, and we went inside to check in.

There were only a handful of tense patients in the waiting room anticipating their name being called to be prepped for surgery, and their groggy, tired family members clutching cups of coffee. My name was finally called. Tired, hungry, and scared, I was directed to a separate room and instructed to change into a hospital gown and lie down. Soon the room was buzzing with activity, with the nurses coming in and out checking my vitals, and the anesthesiologist asking me questions about whether or not I was allergic to certain drugs, and how I might feel upon wakening from the anesthetic, and the breast surgeon reassuring me, going over the procedure, and then the plastic surgeon came in to do the same. Each one also required me to sign a permission slip to have the surgery. Laurie and Buzz sat with me the whole time. We said a prayer together, and then, I was wheeled into surgery.

Hours later, feeling groggy, I tried with great difficulty to open my eyes.

Where am I, I wondered.

As my eyes began to focus, I remembered the operation. I awoke in a small, white room, by myself, surrounded by murmuring machines. There was no window, only low artificial light. I noticed that I could not move, and I felt there were needles in my arms, and I noticed three large tubes with a rubber bulb attached to each end were connected to my armpit. I was aware of a dull aching pain on my left side.

After a few minutes, a nurse entered to check on me and to read the machines.

"You are doing well. Would you like to see your sister and husband?"

I nodded. She bustled out and immediately Laurie came in as Buzz was in the cafeteria getting them sandwiches. Despite my grogginess, I was desperate to know the status and questioned my sister, "Did they find cancer in my lymph nodes? Has it spread? Were they able to remove all the cancer from my breast?"

In a soft, measured voice, Laurie, calmly and quickly assured me, "They removed all the cancer. Your margins are clean. Dr. Valerie, the breast surgeon, checked and rechecked. The plastic surgery went really well, too. However, they did find cancer in the sentinel node, so they removed sixteen more nodes from your armpit."

She paused before she finished the rest, as she knew what it would mean to me. "Of the sixteen lymph nodes they removed, they found three that contained cancer."

My heart fell. I knew this meant that the oncologist would recommend chemotherapy. My thoughts ran head-on into the grogginess – *How could I possibly do chemotherapy again? How could my body survive another assault from those toxins?*

The darkness enveloped me again.

Over the next few weeks, as I healed from surgery, my emotions constantly flipped back and forth. One moment I felt safe and loved by God, and the next I was furiously screaming at God. Sometimes I just surrendered to God. Other times I panicked, not knowing what God wanted from me.

I implored God in my prayers and meditations, in my journal writing, to help me see. *What insights do I need to be aware of? What do I need to let go of?* Fearful that I might miss something, I continued my perfectionistic pattern, trying hard to do everything right. I went in and out, railing at God.

What lesson must I learn this time? What if I don't learn the lesson and the cancer keeps coming back?

One day, several weeks after the surgery, as I stared out the window with my heart pounding, I asked God in a soft, quiet tone, "Will I learn my lesson? Will I learn what I need to know from having breast cancer? Will I pass this time? Will I get an A? B? C? F?"

Suddenly, I realized that I have measured my life by passes and failures – grades. Who I am is wrapped up in passing and failing. Breast cancer was another test. I wondered why am I afraid if I do not have or know the right answers? Somewhere along the way, I must have been terribly shamed for not having the right answers.

When my wounds from surgery healed, I needed to make a decision. Standard treatment for breast cancer is surgery; then after you are healed, chemotherapy, radiation, and a drug called Arimidex for postmenopausal women when the tumor is estrogen-driven. I had a fearful aversion to taking chemotherapy again. As if my body was saying, *'Please no.'* At the time, my sister's research reported that, in general, for breast cancer, chemotherapy increases the odds of the cancer not returning by only six percent. Is six percent worth the trauma to my body, again?

I was hanging by a thread. My emotions were raw – underneath was a boiling cauldron of rage, sadness, and fear. One day I would make up my mind and say "No, no more chemotherapy. I will go an alternative healing path" and the next day, pressured by my oncologist, and friends, I wonder, "What if I am one of the six percent chemotherapy helps?"

I change my mind. Again.

Then, one morning after a heavy snowfall, I awoke to a bright and sunny day. My heart lifted as I soaked in the white snow silhouetted against an azure sky. Walking into the kitchen intent on preparing breakfast for my hungry girls, I glanced out the large sliding glass window, which overlooked the back yard. I saw a bright red color zigzagging through the snow with a slight movement on the ground. Looking closer, I saw an injured rabbit, hampered by the deep snow, bleeding and struggling to get away from our dog.

I burst into sobs, screaming for my husband.

"Buzz, I need help! She's dying, she's dying!"

Terrified by the sound of my voice, my husband and daughters quickly came running. All I could do was point at the rabbit and plead to the three of them "Please! Help her!"

My family had no idea why I was so upset, after all Chase, our German Short Hair had killed other animals without me reacting like this. Eyeing me rather strangely, everyone did what they could to help the rabbit. Mindy ran to find a box to confine the rabbit. Buzz and Alyce ran outside to separate Chase from the rabbit. Of course, it was too late. The rabbit was dead.

Even I was surprised by my reaction. Later that day, writing in my journal, it became clear to me that as I saw the rabbit struggling to survive, I became the rabbit, terrified, helpless, alone, and struggling to make another life-and-death decision, the victim/angry part of me railing at God about having cancer again.

After weeks of agonizing, I decided to do chemotherapy again. Maybe I would be one of the six women out of one hundred that would be helped. Due to the severe toxicity of the chemotherapy drugs I took for non-Hodgkin's lymphoma, I could not repeat them, even though some of those drugs were the top choice for breast cancer. The oncology team at Northwestern decided upon a different chemotherapy cocktail: CMF (Cytoxan, Methotrexate, and Fluorouracil), which would not be quite as toxic. I decided once again, to include in my treatment Chinese herbs, a modified macrobiotic diet, acupuncture, meditation, and yoga.

Once I made this decision, my spirit felt lighter. I listened to Dean Martin singing 'Sway,' a terrific rumba. I started to dance, feeling happy and alive. I thought, *I will not stop dancing my life. I will not allow the fear of cancer returning to color my days and nights, sucking out the joy of living. I will not allow the darkness of the unknown as to when, where or how a cancer may return to keep me from dancing.* I wrote in my journal:

> *Today, I say stop. Enough. What is, is. I can focus on dying or living, the choice is mine. As before, I will trust that God will lead me to where I need to be. I will surrender to mystery, trusting I will be taken care of no matter what happens.*

With the breast surgery over and the incisions healed, and feeling more positive after the decision to do chemotherapy again, I called and made an appointment to see Barbara, the psychotherapist specializing in Jungian dream analysis. It was time to explore the Asian Man Dream that had been haunting me.

Chapter 16 – The Wisdom of the Dream

*"Yesterday I was clever, so I wanted to change the world. Today I am
wise, so I am changing myself."*
~Rumi

I had no problem finding Barbara's office, which was
in her home several miles from where I lived. I was curious
about her office being in her home and wondered *how does
that work?* During our initial phone conversation, she
pleasantly explained, "When you arrive, just come in the front
door without knocking. I'll be with a client upstairs in my
office. When I'm finished, I'll come and get you." She went
on to say, "There is a closet in the entry. Feel free to hang your
coat and then take a seat on one of the chairs in the foyer."

During that conversation, I had shared with her a short
synopsis on what was going on in my life and the reason I
wanted her help, after which she agreed to see me.

I arrived a little early since this was my first time and
I followed her instructions. While waiting for her to fetch me,
I began to feel a little apprehensive about sharing this crazy
dream. *What would she think about me? How screwed up am
I? Will this dream reveal deep, dark secrets?*

I did not have long to wait. Barbara came downstairs
with her earlier client and cheerfully bid him farewell. Then
she turned and warmly greeted me, shaking my hand, "How
wonderful to meet you. I'm Barbara. It appears you found my
house all right."

I smiled and said, "Yes," feeling more at ease with her
genuine welcome.

She looked to be in her late thirties, dressed in a killer cream, tailored suit with heels to match. She had long black hair tied back with a barrette and a lovely smile. I thought how classy and professional she looked.

After pointing out the restroom, she asked if I would like a glass of water. I declined and then, clutching my journal, I proceeded to follow her slim figure upstairs. After closing the office door behind me, she motioned for me to sit in a comfortable chair across from hers. Sunlight filled the room coming from a large window behind her desk. Along one wall, walnut shelves held many books with small objects of art interspersed. On another pale blue wall hung all her degrees, tastefully framed.

Everything about Barbara was elegant; her movements were slow and graceful even as she crossed one leg over the other. Holding a clipboard in her lap with a yellow pad attached, she spoke in a kind, caring voice, "I understand you have some challenging health issues. I certainly hope I am able to help." Then, thinking for a moment, she continued, "Maybe it would help if you would explain your goal, what you expect from this visit."

Encouraged, I shared my history about the first cancer and now, five years later, I was dealing with another cancer diagnosis. She shook her head with empathy and concern. I went on, "Very soon after the second cancer diagnosis I had an extremely vivid, terrifying dream. In my gut, I know this is an important and significant dream." I paused, not wanting to sound too dramatic, but I added, "A life or death dream."

Barbara nodded as if she understood completely. As a specialist in Jungian dream analysis, she really did. With her soft brown eyes totally focused on mine, she placed a strand of loose hair behind her ear and leaned toward me waiting for me to begin. I opened my journal and began to read.

I am a therapist, counseling a middle-aged Asian man in my home. My office is upstairs, with steps leading to my office on the outside of the house. I knew the sound of his step as he slowly shuffled up the stairs. The man was deeply depressed and had a difficult life. During our counseling session, he suddenly reached for me and pulled out my left breast (which was the breast with the cancer) and began to nurse - as if his need was life or death.

I allowed it, but was uncomfortable. I understood his desperation. I saw him again on another occasion. This time I was only clad in a bra. And he nursed again. I knew he would expect to nurse every time. I knew this was a gross crossing of boundaries. It was not sexual. It was a deep need of his to nurse.

In the next dream scene, while still in my bra, a woman neighbor across the street, one who was a famous decorator, invited me over. Wearing only my bra and slacks I wrapped myself in a blanket and walked over. Proud and pleased, she showed me her decorating work. She had long curtains hiding a 'wall view' of another building. A floral screen print covered her dining room walls with a rug to match on the floor. She glanced at me with curiosity and asked me, 'What do you have on underneath the blanket?' I pulled open the blanket and she was shocked to see that I was only

195

wearing a bra. She furrowed her brow and gave me a side-glance. Clearly, she was judging me about what I was doing with my Asian client.

Barbara listened attentively, taking a few notes. After I finished sharing the dream, she had questions and insights for me to consider, reminding me that objects and people in our dreams symbolize parts of ourselves.

Could the Asian man, being dark and foreign, symbolize my shadow side, the part of me that I hide in my unconscious mind, too afraid and ashamed to own?

- The Asian man also comes in disguise as cancer, inappropriately taking control, invading my boundaries.
- Cancer is invasive; however, if the cancer does not feed off of me it will die.
- How are males invasive in my life and how do I allow for that?
- The creative woman in my dream (me) knows what is happening.

In order to work through these issues, Barbara asked me to rewrite the dream and set boundaries. At the time, I thought it was a strange request, however, I complied with the 'homework.' Sitting at home, I began the rewrite:

I am a therapist counseling an Asian man. For the last two sessions I have allowed him to nurse on my left breast and I know this must stop. I could hear his footsteps coming up the stairs, very slow and deliberate. As he opened the door, I saw again the desperation on his face. His demeanor had not changed: pathetic, sad eyes; his body language weak and slow. He began to walk toward me and I said, "Stop!"

He sat down and before he could speak of how much he needed me, I said firmly, "I cannot see you anymore. What I allowed you to do (nurse) was totally inappropriate, a gross transgression of boundaries for me as a therapist and a human being. I apologize for allowing the behavior, for my part in what happened, but it will not happen again and you must leave my office, my life, now! I will not see you again under any circumstances. I resent your pathetic excuses for your leech-like behavior and you will not suck my energy for one more second! There is the door!"

He looked shocked at my words, and for a moment it seemed as if he would try to change my mind, but looking at my face, he could see there was no point. He almost seemed afraid of me as he quickly took his leave.

As he descended the stairs and drove away, I felt relieved, lighter and free. Sitting in my office, revelling in my assertiveness and power, my neighbor called and asked me to come over and see her new decorating. She was beautifully dressed and complimented me on my business suit, 'elegant and professional.'

Over a cup of tea, she said, "I can see you have changed. You appear stronger, more peaceful and more assured." She had seen the Asian man quickly leave and I knew she understood what had just happened. She then showed me her living room, her latest decorating accomplishment, which was painted a beautiful, buttery, soft yellow with cream trim. There was a lovely picture hanging on a prominent wall. It was of a woman, sitting on large, white wicker chair in her backyard, having tea. She was peacefully reading a book with her feet tucked under her long dress. Her stone house was in the background covered with yellow wisteria climbing the walls, surrounded by a lush green lawn and trees.

The picture I described in the dream re-write actually hung on my living room wall, a recent gift from my sister, Laurie. I remembered thinking, *I want to be that woman,* but wondered – *Would I ever be that peaceful? Could I ever be that relaxed knowing all that lay before me now?*

Nevertheless, encouraged by rewriting this dream, I saw the power pour on to the page. At first, I wondered where it came from. Then, reading the rewrite to Barbara at my next appointment gave me a sense of empowerment and relief. I felt freer, less shackled, as if a momentous shift had taken place. In the rewrite I had found my voice, I spoke with authority, set firm boundaries – *No means No!* and told the cancer, (aka the Asian Man,) to leave. I was no longer some poor helpless victim. I admit I have little control over what happens in my life at times, but *I do have a choice as to how I will respond to life's challenges.* I can hide under a rock, pretending nothing happened, or I can accept what *is* – trusting that God and I can handle each trial set before me. I do have a choice – will I choose (as Carolyn Myss would say) "wisdom?" or "woe?" I chose the path of wisdom.

Looking at myself in the dream as the therapist, I wanted to rescue the Asian Man. He had asked for help, what was wrong with that intention? Nothing on the face of it, but I cannot rescue anyone without considering my own well-being and never by sacrificing my integrity.

I reflected further on Barbara's comment about the Asian Man being dark and foreign symbolizing parts of my shadow side. *How am I, like the Asian Man, perpetrating violence on others?* At first, I wanted to erase this question from my mind with – *I would never do anything like that – I am kind and loving toward others!* However, I soon realized that judgmental and critical thoughts were really a part of my thinking when others didn't meet my moral standards. Judgments toward other people are toxic. I also recognized this tendency to persecute and judge myself unmercifully when I felt I did not measure up in some way.

The wisdom of the dream asked me another very important question via Barbara, 'How are males invasive in your life and why do you allow for that?' Pondering this question during one of our counseling sessions, I explained, "From a very early age I tried hard to squeeze affirmation from the male population that I do measure up, that I am smart and pretty enough – everything I wanted from my father, but never received enough of. And as a consequence, I allowed my personal space to be invaded by agreeing with and allowing actions that were not what I wanted – too afraid to have a voice for fear of being rejected." For example, I remembered times when I was dating and kissing dates goodnight or making out because I *owed* them in some way or if I didn't, they would think less of me.

If every part of this dream was about me - *How was I like the famous decorator in the dream?* Like her, I was creative, intuitive and smart. She saw and understood everything. As if she were my conscience, she asked, "What are you doing? Your behavior with the Asian Man will not bring healing and wholeness to anyone."

On our last session together, Barbara helped me to see the Asian Man was not all evil. From her perspective, it was clear the Asian man helped me see the truth of my weakness in allowing others to move into my personal space, which led me on a path to discover that no one, male or female, has the power to name who I am, or make decisions for me. This dream reinforced the lessons I was already learning on my healing path, which included taking responsibility for my behavior and stop blaming others, having realistic expectations and forgiving others and myself often. And most importantly nurturing and practicing self-care of my body, mind and spirit.

Ironically, so far on my healing journey, I had already encountered several Asians, two men and one woman who were profoundly helpful. It was an Asian doctor who first diagnosed the cancer, an Asian surgeon who correctly biopsied the tissue and an Asian herbalist who helped me heal from the toxic drugs.

These were powerful insights that helped me further on my path to healing and wholeness. I read and mused over the re-write, making the dream as to how I wanted to see myself in real life, such as, setting healthy boundaries, creating beauty and making positive life choices. I could actually see myself becoming that woman.

Barbara mentioned several times that there were many levels to dreams, and that we had not exhausted the insights from this dream. But, feeling greatly relieved and grounded in the power and the insights the rewrite had already given me, I knew it was now time to focus my energy on chemotherapy – again.

Chapter 17– Chemotherapy Again

"The problem is not the problem; the imagined tyranny of the problem is the problem."
~James Finley

Ann told me that every time I had chemotherapy, she would have a surprise package waiting for me. She mailed them to the oncology department and each time I was hooked up to the chemotherapy drugs, a nurse would hand me a beautifully wrapped box. Her thoughtfulness made the chemotherapy bearable. Even with that, the four months of chemotherapy passed very slowly. I kept falling into wells of depression and could not give words to the depth of fear, anger, and sadness. I often filled my sad and fearful times with activity, doing the dishes, laundry, watching TV, reading, journaling – anything other than stopping a moment to feel the sadness or fear.

The ongoing ticker tape flowing through my mind kept telling me that I am defective. But the sad truth is everyone believes they are defective one way or another because none of us were loved perfectly. This negative feeling left me with a sense of separation and alienation – a pervasive, energetic heaviness. Strongly believing in the interconnectedness of body/mind/spirit, I knew I had to change this invasive message – *I am defective.* Surely, my negative thinking played into the formation of the cancer cells, because by nature cancer cells are defective.

Thinking of my negative focus, I considered one day – *Do I get my ego needs met by being the 'great' sick person? Do I have to be sick to get what I need? Do I have a death wish?* These thoughts were as horrifying to me then – as they were when I recognized them five years earlier with the diagnosis of lymphoma. I thought I was done with that pattern, but I could not run from this awareness. Standing in front of a huge mirror in my living room, I looked at myself and said over and over, "I do not need to be sick to get my needs met. I do not need to be sick to get my needs met ... I am enough. I am enough."

Halfway through chemotherapy I journaled:

I am tired, tired of my thoughts about cancer, getting well, death, dying, even my spiritual books don't help. I feel so stuck with these repetitive themes, ruminating over and over in my mind along with tinnitus, which causes a constant ringing in my ears. Traditional Chinese Medicine would say tinnitus means my kidneys are low on Qi (energy, life force); so, I am reminded every moment how my body is struggling with chemotherapy, again.

I was aware of a part of me yearning to be free. Free to do whatever I want. Whenever and however I want. Free from the responsibility of child-raising. Free from working so hard to get well. Free from concerns about money. Free from the fear of living and dying. Free from the 'sick' persona. Free from explaining how I am feeling and doing every day. I wondered, since I wanted to run away how in the world does Buzz feel? He must have thought about running away. But, I was too tired to ask him or discuss it with him.

My hair did not fall out like the first chemotherapy; however, it was thin everywhere. I wondered if it would come back thick, like it did the first time. My husband still likes the thin pubic section. "A turn-on," he says. It's unfortunate my libido has taken a powder; my sexual drive is nonexistent. I wonder if I will ever find it again? If this low libido continues during the radiation part of treatment, my Chinese herbal specialist would give me a 'thumbs up.' Traditional Chinese Medicine recommends having intercourse only once a month during radiation treatment to keep all your energy for healing. That is a directive I could easily follow!

Finally, as winter slowly passed, I began to see signs of spring. One day, with spring approaching, I looked deeply out my bedroom window, where I meditated. Every morning, I looked for green, which appeared first in the grass, becoming less and less brown. In the woods, I saw small shoots of daffodil leaves growing taller and taller. Scilla, one of the first flowers of spring, broke through the frozen soil and quickly bloomed with bright blue blossoms. Every day I observed the trees and bushes, noticing their swollen buds, and soon, I began to see the soft, pale green, marking the beginning – their *coming forth*. My heart would beat faster. I wondered what fruit would come forth this spring? What flowers? That spring day held excitement and expectation of the gifts that would come from this long dark winter. I did not have long to wait.

In late spring, as I was drawing near to the end of chemotherapy, over one weekend I received many unexpected gifts.

- I was delighted and thrilled when, Friday evening, Mindy attended her first prom as a junior in high school. She tingled with excitement as she stepped into her sparkly, blue dress and put the finishing touches to her curly hair in an *updo*.
- I was humbled and speechless. Abby said she wanted to have a garage sale for me. I thought – *How*

wonderful and thoughtful of her. I will have an extra several hundred dollars on hand to help pay for costs insurance did not cover. There were many costs, as insurance still did not pay for any alternative treatments that helped boost my immune system.

On the day of the sale I was a little embarrassed to be the focus of attention. I stopped over at the sale to thank everyone – many friends and family were helping, even my mother! At the end of the day, Abby and my other sisters, and sister-in-law, Robin, came over to my house and presented me with a box. Abby said, "You will never guess how much is in there!" The box was full of money; all counted and tallied – $9,000! Never in my wildest dreams did I think they could make $9,000! It turns out many people from different churches donated items.

- I was joyful. My good friend Maureen came down from Madison to help with the garage sale and the next day we went to the local flea market.
- I was comforted. My wonderful mother-in-law, Mary, visited from Florida. As always, as soon as she walked in the door, she asked, "How can I help you?"

So many gifts to be grateful for – people had come to my aid, many without my even asking, as they had with the first cancer. I was again humbled by everyone's expressions of love and generosity.

With the money from the garage sale, a huge financial burden had lifted. I was happy and ready to face the next treatment – which would be an entire summer of radiation, every day, except the weekends.

Chapter 18 – The Purifying Fire of Radiation

"I haven't a clue how my story will end, but that's all right. When you set out on a journey and night covers the road, that's when you discover the stars."
~Nancy Willard

Helen, a friend from my church community, called me late one night after she heard about the breast cancer diagnosis. A breast cancer survivor herself, she encouraged me and strongly recommended Dr. Bill Small, an oncology radiologist from Northwestern, who happened to be her neighbor. Helen, a former nurse, is a force to be reckoned with, outspoken, forceful in her opinions, but extraordinarily kind. With her New York accent she insisted, "You *must* see Bill. Call him. Call him at home right now. Here is his number."

Equally forceful, I protested, "Oh no, I can't call him now. It's too late! And calling him at home? No, no, I couldn't."

Helen, persisted, *"No, call him right now.* I promise you it's okay."

I hung up from Helen and called Bill. True to her word, he couldn't have been more sympathetic and gracious with his kind reassuring words, "Don't worry, we will take care of you. Call my office to schedule an appointment. Should you have any problems, ask to speak with me."

Right then, I decided when chemotherapy was over, I would make the trip into Chicago every day to put myself in the care of this kind, highly recommended oncology radiologist who, upon meeting, looked like he was twelve years old. I spent the summer receiving radiation.

Taking the train into the city on the first day with Laurie, I felt a wave of gratitude sweep over me. Still floating on the relief that chemotherapy was over and that I had health insurance, grateful for my life, for my gardens, my husband, children, a loving extended family, and friends. The day was warm and sunny. There were people of all ages headed into the city for work, or to have fun sightseeing or playing hooky to attend a Cub's baseball game. *Life is good.*

I wondered just how bad could this radiation possibly be? Laurie had discovered in her research that radiating the breast provided the highest percentage of success for the cancer not returning.

My heart began to beat a little faster as we entered the radiation center, which was deep in the bowels of the hospital. We stepped off the elevator and saw a room full of people waiting for their name to be called. I signed in and sat down. For a room full of people, the room was quiet. People talked in hush tones. Fear, sadness and vulnerability permeated the room.

The first day of radiation is the day that you are measured and 'marked' with a tiny tattoo mark, the size of a pencil point so the radiologist will know exactly where to put the stream of radiation. They finally called my name and I was shown to a row of lockers and instructed to undress and put on a short robe.

I was then led to the radiation room. There were no windows, low lighting and several large formidable machines. From under one of the larger machines, the technician rolled out an x-ray table. She took my elbow and guided me onto the table. Lying there in the darkened room, the technician said kindly, but forcefully, "Hold your left arm over your head. *Do not move anything* until we are finished measuring and marking your skin. It is imperative that you do not move so we can get the correct measurement. This may take as long as an hour."

With my left arm over my head, beginning to tingle and go numb, I stared at the ceiling tiles, thinking *this can't be me. What am I doing in this alien place? How can I have breast cancer?*

As if someone had just turned on a faucet, tears began to roll down my cheeks. Somehow my body knew how to cry the tears of grief while holding me completely still. The nurses saw me in my sorrow and silently from time to time wiped away my tears.

When the marking was finally over, my young-looking doctor came over and was surprised to see me crying. He asked me, "Why are you crying? The procedure is over."

The next day, while in the waiting room for my second treatment, I noticed a little boy about six years old, bald with a huge lump on his head, being wheeled into the waiting room in a three-wheel carriage. The woman who was pushing him also had a baldhead. As they parked next to me, I wondered *who is the patient?*

I said, "Hello," and introduced myself to the woman who informed me her name was Sue and this was her little boy, Oliver, "Ollie" for short. In solidarity, to support her son, Sue had shaved her head. By the firm set of her jaw, she was fighting for her child's life, but I could see dread and panic in her eyes. She was torn between staying positive with a warrior's stance, doing everything possible to save her boy's life and aware of the crushing possibility that her child might die.

Sue shared that Ollie had seven more weeks of radiation for a brain tumor. When she needed to visit the washroom, I told her I would keep an eye on Ollie. After she left, I said softly, "Hi, Ollie. How old are you?" He turned his head away from me and began to cry. I wasn't sure if I had scared him or if he missed his mother, his constant rock. I wished I had said, *Oh, Ollie, I feel like crying, too.*

On the train ride home, I thought about that little guy and his Mom and felt sad, grateful, and angry and then made a pact with myself, *if Ollie can do this for seven weeks, so can I. We have a shared humanity.*

Receiving radiation became a rather smooth routine. After a week of juggling times and deciding whether to take the train or drive, always testing which was faster or less stressful, Laurie and I decided to take the train three times a week and drive the other two days. That way, I could see a chiropractor for alternative treatments. Laurie dropped everything to go with me each day. As the summer wore on, my other sisters took turns going with us. Treatment and travel took about four hours each day. That is half a day. Everyday. Clearly, if I was to have any life at all, I would need to be asleep by 10 p.m. and up at 6 a.m. That way I'd be ready to leave by 8 a.m. Recognizing this was my life, I was pleased with the schedule:

- do small picking up
- move water hoses
- make teas
- make veggie juice and clean up
- eat breakfast
- take supplementary pills
- meditate

The dressing rooms in the radiation oncology department were unisex. In each small dressing room there were three lockers where patients could hang their clothes.

Sometimes, when I came out of the dressing room there were several men in similar green hospital gowns waiting to be called for treatment in the room next to mine. We all looked the same. Naked and helpless beneath our green gowns.

One day, I noticed an elderly man with gray hair and large glasses. He was small in stature and walked with a limp. His glasses made his eyes look huge. He kept walking back and forth with a lost look on his face, trying to locate the dressing room. When I came back from being *zapped* with radiation, I realized that the dressing room where I had left my clothes was locked. I sat down and waited, assuming someone would open the door shortly. The same elderly gentleman finally came out looking disoriented, especially when he saw me going into the same dressing room. When I opened my locker, I saw he had hung his pants and underwear over my blouse and bra. All I could do was laugh. Later I learned the radiation room next to mine radiated all the prostate cancer patients. We were being attacked in private, sexual areas, all of us vulnerable, scared, and disoriented.

During the middle of radiation treatment, just when I was feeling overwhelmed with the everyday trek into Chicago, out of the blue, I received a thin envelope from my mother's brother, Bernard, my sweet 'Uncle Nard.' Throughout his life, 'Unc' was an avid letter writer. But now in his eighties and since his wife, Ruth, died he rarely wrote letters any more. We spoke on the phone every few weeks.

In my bedroom, sitting on the bed I opened the envelope and unfolded a piece of thin lined paper taken from a small, spiral notebook. A check made out to me fell to the floor. There were two sentences written on the piece of paper which said:

Dear Debby,

Eileen, [his niece by marriage] John [Eileen's husband] and I were sitting here doing nothing and we decided to send you a check. We all love you and pray for you.

Love, Unc

I picked up the check from the floor. I thought it said $100.00 and then realized that it had been written for $10,000. I cried and cried.

Memories welled up inside me. I remembered my father screaming and swearing at me when I asked him for money. He yelled, "Goddamn it, don't you know? Money doesn't grow on trees!" And then he would begrudgingly give me the money. Seeing myself through Dad's eyes, I didn't feel worth much. But then my Uncle sends me $10,000. When I called to thank him, crying, he said gently, "Deb, it's only money and not worth your tears." I could only say *Thank you*, over and over.

One day toward the end of radiation treatment, I decided to go into the city alone. I just wanted the silence. My radiologist had informed me that I would need ten more booster shots to the former tumor site in my breast, and also into the lymph nodes up my neck and back. Thinking I was finished with treatment, sadness crept over me. It is difficult to explain what it feels like to hurt a part of your body, to see it become tender and red, more burned every day. I whispered to my radiated body, *It's okay. You are doing wonderfully. I'm sorry to hurt you. Angels are protecting you.*

When I received energy healing (which is really prayer) from my dear friends, they spoke of purifying the body under the fire of radiation. I reminded myself of this every day. It kept me focused on the treatment as positive.

During this time another positive force entered my life. The LivingWell Cancer Resource Center, (LWCRC) opened close to where I lived and offered support and education classes free to any cancer patient. At first, I did not want their help. I did not want to be around other 'sick' people to remind me how sick I was – again. However, I was struggling to stay calm and confident about the efficacy of treatment. I needed support and encouragement from people who understood exactly the grief and sadness that settled into my spirit.

I began to attend the breast cancer support group at LWCRC toward the end of breast cancer treatment. It was here they announced the beginning of a breast cancer yoga group scheduled to meet once a week. The group consisted of about fifteen women, who like myself, had never done yoga before. I had read that yoga focused on the whole person – body, mind and spirit, which greatly appealed to me.

Sitting cross-legged with her back erect, Marianne, the yoga teacher, gave us instruction. In a soft, gentle voice she began each class asking us to set an intention for our practice, such as, letting go of fear, or becoming more flexible, or more trusting, and so on. This activity helped us quiet and focus the mind, which in turn, calmed our bodies. Moving into each pose we were often reminded to let go of our thoughts and focus on the present moment. Throughout the session she would explain every movement and the benefit from that movement, such as how a particular stretch helped the liver or cleansed the lymph nodes. Her clarifications helped me stay motivated and present. The session always ended with a relaxation that further calmed the body, mind and spirit.

In the past, I was not very gentle with myself in any area of my life. The yoga experience reinforced the importance of using my breath to calm myself, to pay attention to how I was breathing. The gentle way the instructors helped us move our bodies into different poses – not in a quick hurried fashion – but slowly, and with purpose and encouragement gave us constant reminders to be kind to ourselves. I felt my body and spirit respond to this kindness. We were taught to pay attention to our bodies and bring light and healing to the places that were tight and stressed. At times, Marianne would take the time to allow us to introduce ourselves and say one thing positive about our life or some other short directive. We began to get to know one another and become supportive as we shared, and recognized we were very similar in our fears and struggles. I wrote in my journal:

Today I reflected on the women in my breast cancer yoga group. Last night, we laughed and talked about missing breasts and scarred chests, finding bras that didn't 'slip up,' breasts that were lopsided, nerves that had been cut causing numbness, pocket bras that were filled with soft silicon and felt unbelievably real. How is this possible to laugh and joke about such a thing? A memory flashed through my head of the heart palpitating fear I felt thinking of the possibility of having breast cancer years before I was even diagnosed. And now, here I am with these beautiful, brave women laughing. How did I come so far? How did we all come so far? Amazing Grace.

.

Chapter 19 – To Bee or Not to Be?

"I do not have to go to Sacred Places in far-off lands. The ground I stand on is holy... And I toil and sweat and watch and wonder and I am full of love. Living in place in this place. For truth and beauty dwell here."
~Mary de La Valette

It was early August and I was going through the last few weeks of radiation. The weather had been hot, but we were catching a few eighty-degree days. This was one of those cool days – a good time to tend to the weeds in the rose garden. After working for a while, I rested on a flat rock contemplating the roses, one of my favorite flowers.

What an enigma. As hybrids, these roses were frustrating to grow. All the work with fertilizer, mulch, winter protection, pruning, fighting off insects and diseases, and then, the thorns that scratch and wound. But what beauty! The infinite varieties of shape, form, and color. The indescribable aroma that fills every pore of your being, and just for a moment, you experience heaven. The velvet touch of a rose petal is like a baby's soft cheek. They are worth the effort. Every function I have performed for these roses, God has done for me. And more.

While resting there on the rock, a bee buzzed around my head and settled on a pale, pink David Austin Rose. The flowers' spicy aroma filled my senses. My mind flashed to the Hebrew meaning of my name, Deborah, which is *bee. How appropriate*, I thought. *Before cancer, I was just like this bee, buzzing around frantically running from flower to flower. 'To bee or not to be' was the question for the day and every day.*

Can I really learn the earth lesson from the rose? To be? Rather than just do?

That night I experienced a dream:

I'm gardening. I pick up a huge pile of weeds and place them in a garbage bag. As I haul the bag to be discarded, I look down at my hand and see my emerald engagement ring is missing. Horrified, I remembered it was on my finger before weeding. Frantically, I emptied the garbage bag full of weeds, throwing everything on the ground. There it was! Sparkling, the emerald was among the weeds. But where was the setting? Pawing through the weeds on the ground I finally found the setting. I let out a sigh of relief.

Still feeling relief upon wakening, I quickly wrote down the dream.

I began to consider the correlation between weeding the garden and weeding myself of negative thoughts and feelings. *What else was I purging and weeding from my life?* Physically, I was cleansing my body of cancer through radiation, and, spiritually I was learning the importance of present moment living. Living in the *now* could take root in a healthy body coupled with conscious awareness.

Whenever there is illness, there is loss. Through the dream, my soul said I could find what had been lost. The ring I lost and then found symbolized my True Self, the treasure hidden in the field, or the pearl of great price of which Jesus speaks. Before cancer, I was lost in the frantic doing of life, trying to measure up and be perfect, losing my True Self in a frantic pace to belong. How paradoxical the dream showed me finding my True Self in the weeds ready to be pitched into the garbage. My dream revealed messages that marked the way to health and wholeness. Dreams are not a foreign, forgotten language! Dreams are messages from the wisdom of our soul.

This dream buoyed my spirits while I completed the final weeks of radiation. I would soon face another health decision.

My joy and relief of completing radiation was soon replaced with confusion, fear, anger, sadness, and even rebellion. Since I was post-menopausal, the oncology doctors wanted me to take a new drug called Arimidex. This is a drug that inhibits the production of estrogen. *Would I dry up like a prune? What happens to a woman who has no estrogen? Will I be hounded by hot flashes?* I felt rebellious and angry. *Why do I have to deal with this? My friends are happily planning trips, retirement, and children's weddings – and I'm dealing with cancer again and all the after-effects!* Feeling like a victim, again…

Even though radiation was over, my oncologist wanted to meet with me. I dragged myself to our last meeting.

"As of today, you are cancer free."

"How do you know?" I said. He shrugged his shoulders.

"Based on your treatment, we see no more cancer."

I did love hearing this news, but I knew – and he knew – that no one knows for sure.

Thus, began a new chapter of learning to dance with cancer.

I felt myself awakening as if from a deep sleep. Feelings of joy, enthusiasm, and expectation began to surface like long lost friends. I felt like Jonah in the belly of the whale, floundering in the ocean in darkness and suddenly finding myself washed up on the beach, exhausted and confused not knowing which way to go, or what to do first. Feeling the warmth of the sun and blinded, at first by the light— immobilized and exhausted. The long haul of treatment was finally over and now I could rest and dream of what I wanted to bring in to my life.

For two weeks after seeing Dr. Small, I stayed close to home basking in the light and freedom from treatment. Then, questions begin to surface. *As my hair grows back, will the cancer come back? How do I keep track of two cancers? What do I do now to stay healthy? What will be the long-term effects of Arimidex? What alternative therapies do I continue?*

Alternative supplements are expensive and time consuming. My friends, Anger, Fear, and Worry, began to keep me company – again, making my hold on Presence tenuous. None of us are alone in this struggle. St. Theresa of the Little Flower came to my aid, saying in her book, about herself:

> *... nothing surprises me anymore, and I am not distressed when my helplessness is brought home to me; on the contrary, I make it my boast, and expect each day to reveal some imperfection which I had not seen before.*

I found solace in my sacred place, where I meditate and breathe; also, in the stillness of Nature I found Presence and Peace.

Soon after radiation was over, I knew it was time. *How can you not check your breasts when you have told all your beloved women friends and family how important this is?*

I took a deep breath and pictured the warrior woman on the breast cancer postage stamp and for the first time I began to medically examine my breasts. Fear magnified every irregular, lumpy area, of which there were many. Now, I was certain I had felt a lump. For weeks I had put off this daunting task, leaving it to the doctors. I could not face finding another lump.

Breathe, I remind myself. *In one week, I will have a checkup for lymphoma so I can have my breast checked then. Thank God.*

In the meantime, what could I do? Nothing. I went to my sacred place and read a quote by Thich Nhat Hanh in a journal given to me by a dear friend:

> *"Our true home is in the present moment.*
> *When we enter the present moment deeply,*
> *our regrets and sorrows disappear and*
> *we discover life with all its wonders."*

I remembered the words of Jesus in Matthew 6:25, "Be anxious for nothing."

These words were a balm to my soul. I made a decision not to give myself over to what might be and enjoyed the day.

"Everything is fine," my doctor assured me one week later, "Normal breasts will feel like cauliflower."

I realized, once again, learning to dance in the dark takes practice. I was still learning the basic steps. Some days dancing effortlessly with grace and joy; other days I practiced the same step over and over, with frustration and angst that I will never learn the dance, and with Fear as my constant partner.

So, every day, and sometimes every moment, I chose the joy of living as my partner, and took comfort in this universal dance. I basked in the warmth of God's love for me, manifesting itself in the ineffable beauty of my family, friends, and Nature. And I rejoiced.

Chapter 20 – From the Fire into the Garden

"When you step into Nature's realm, you are stepping into a place of
awakening, a place where your deepest self can be revealed, including
your spiritual core."
~Nancy Chickerneo

That fall, several months after completing treatment, I returned to work as a psychotherapist in private practice. My mission statement was to help others integrate body, mind and spirit into health and wholeness. And I could authentically help others with confidence because I had 'walked the walk.' At home, as I continued to create more garden spaces, a desire to share Nature with others began to grow.

Thomas Merton said that Nature and animals are in perfect alignment with God's will. It is we as humans who struggle to surrender to God's will. Nature completely yields to God. My attitude opened and yielded to absorbing and learning from Nature what I desired most – surrendering my own will to God's will. This meant not giving up but accepting 'what is' and trusting that life would give me exactly what I needed to learn – all the earth lessons that God would set before me in each present moment. I wanted to yield to God as Nature does.

As I became more conscious, more attuned to using my senses, Nature continued to 'speak' to me about life, God and myself. One summer day, after spending time outside, I asked myself, *How did God attend to me through Nature today? In 'reading' Nature, what did I learn about myself? God? Life?*

How perfectly balanced life was! There was order and beauty everywhere. Everything in Nature was in relationship. Many plants offered food for the birds and animals, in turn;

the birds, insects, and animals spread the seeds, pollinated the flowers and planted nuts. The dead leaves, tree limbs and foliage provided nutrients for the soil. Nothing was wasted.

I saw life-giving trees which offered me shade, soft grass under my feet, patches of dead grass, yet when given water they will thrive, just like human beings when given a drink of kindness and affirmation they will blossom and flourish. Reality is often hidden, composed of the past, present, and future. Dark, fat, blackberries look to be ripe and sweet, yet some of them are not, just like life, which is full of surprises – sometimes sour, sometimes sweet. I came across the body of a chickadee on our deck that looked dead; yet, as I reached down to move the little bird there was a tiny heartbeat. I waited and watched as it regained consciousness and flew away. Perhaps it had flown into a window and was stunned. Humans, like myself, need to be stunned sometimes to wake up to the beauty and gift that surrounds them.

All of the Masters write that deep spiritual transformation comes through suffering. My own life bore witness to this universal truth. Suffering broke down all my ways of coping. I could not make the cancer go away by myself, through prayer or any other way. I was not in control anymore, but forced to let go and move to a deeper, much scarier level of trust. Frustrated, I often asked myself: *Must one always suffer to be transformed? Is that the only way?* The deeper truth stirring in my heart suggested that along with suffering there was another route to transformation – through the path of wonder, aka Nature.

It was my mother who laid the foundation of that truth for me. She saw beauty and wonder in many things: flowers, art, music, sculpture, jewelry, antiques, and Nature. However, her manner of introducing me to beauty and wonder no matter what the object went something like this:

"Debbie, did you see that beautiful flower?"

"Yes, Mom I saw it."

Mom would say, "But did you see the way the light hits the petals? And the shape of the leaves?"

Slightly annoyed, I would tell her, "Yes, Mom I saw it." By this time, I am several paces ahead of her or in the next room thinking the conversation was over.

Raising her voice, she would exclaim, "You *must* come back and see this again – *Look! Look!"*

Of course, she really could see beauty with a sense of wonder and a childlike-spontaneous enthusiasm, but she tried to force it on me. Annoyed by her insistence, I didn't see her wisdom until much later.

Almost every day I thought and reflected – *How could I share this angelic space, so others could connect with the path of wonder through Nature? Would Buzz have any objections? How many days could we be 'open' to the public?* I still had a daughter at home, going to school and my sons were often in and out, discussing business with Buzz. *What about insurance? Could I maintain the upkeep of the gardens? Were they pretty enough?* All of these questions churned inside me for months as I tried to seek a way to make this dream a reality.

About a year after I was in private practice, I received a phone call from Robin, my sister-in-law. Her voice sounded urgent and troubled.

"Deb, I have a request of you. There is a young married mother, who goes to my church with a ten-year old son and a six-year old daughter. She was recently diagnosed with an aggressive, terminal tongue cancer and the family needs help. Would you be willing to help them?"

Without thinking I said, "Of course!"

Later I wondered to myself, questioning what had I agreed to? *How can I possibly help them, especially since the diagnosis was terminal? Would I be an effective therapist after my own diagnosis? Could I be present to them and hold their fear, sorrow and tears without transferring to my own experience?*

On the day I was to meet Melissa and her children, I prayed for guidance, with my heart pounding. I decided I would do an initial interview, like I did with all my clients, to see if we were a good fit. Since this was their first time, I kept watch waiting for their arrival. They soon came down the lane and parked their car. Her ten-year old son bounded out of the car in a short, brown bombardier jacket. He looked up and saw me through the office window and enthusiastically smiled and waved at me. I smiled and waved back, instantly falling in love with this family. Every ounce of fear left me and I knew this would be a perfect fit.

For the next six months, I worked with Melissa and her family helping them through this horrifying diagnosis. Melissa had a childlike faith in God, strong and trusting, and out of that faith and trust, came courage like I had never before witnessed. I helped her write goodbye letters to her children, her husband and family. She even composed a letter that she wanted me to read after the funeral service. Later, someone in her family jokingly told me, "Of course! Melissa *always* wanted to have the last word!"

At the same time, while working with Melissa; the desire to open my gardens to the public became stronger. In the past, as I thought about the possibility, I knew that if the gardens were to open, I wanted to create a memorial garden in honor of our loved ones who have gone from this life into another. After all, what is our spiritual currency? It is love and remembering that love.

During one of her final days, Melissa and I were sitting in her beautiful and tranquil Japanese garden that her husband had created for her, when I decided to share my vision about opening my gardens to the public on certain days. I found myself enthusiastically describing my dream and she loved the idea.

Before I knew it, I said to her, "I am going to open the gardens to the public and I want to create a Memorial Garden with your name on it to honor all of our loved ones. Would you be okay with that?"

Melissa was thrilled. I asked her to name her favorite bird and flower, which were the Indigo Bunting and Calla Lilies. That same day, I called an artist friend of mine, Kathy, to paint a template of the sign that would mark the Memorial Garden. It would say, 'Melissa's Place' with a picture of an Indigo Bunting and Calla Lilies. Kathy had the template of the sign ready to show Melissa that following week, as I had explained the urgency.

The last time I saw Melissa the day was hot and sunny, not a cloud in sight. A terrible drought enveloped Northern Illinois, not a hint of rain for weeks. Melissa greeted me at the front door looking thin and pale. She could barely walk. We sat once again in the welcome shade of the Japanese garden. The waterfall gurgled pleasantly as it flowed over the perfectly placed rocks. It was difficult  for her to speak, but her face lit up when I showed her the sign for her approval. The Indigo Bunting and Calla Lilies were in the center of the sign along with the name of the garden,

'Melissa's Place.' Around the edge of the oval sign was written the last lines of the letter she wrote to her six-year-old daughter, "Draw me a picture, Dance me a dance, Sing me a song." And at the very bottom, I had Kathy write, "Live!"

When it was time for me to leave, Melissa insisted on walking me to the front door. She hugged me goodbye and said in a sweet soft voice, "I hope I see you again."

Melissa died that following week, July of 2005, and the gardens were open to the public in October of that same year.

The day she died rain soaked the parched earth. I thought of Mark Twain and his words: *"Twenty years from now you will be more disappointed – By the things that you didn't do than by the ones you did do. So, throw off the bowlines. Sail away from the safe harbor. Catch the trade winds in your sails. Explore. Dream. Discover."*

Chapter 21 – Healing Gardens

"Nature's peace will flow into you as sunshine flows into trees. The
winds will blow their own freshness into you,
and the storms their energy,
while cares will drop off like autumn leaves."
~John Muir

Upon opening Healing Gardens to the public, our mission became: *to provide a safe, quiet place to experience the Sacred through wooded paths and perennial gardens. We welcome all, honoring each person's faith tradition.* There is no activity required, other than *being* in Nature. At first, on the set Sundays we were open to the public, only three or four people would come. Mom always came and would sit on the front porch with me, where I would greet people and give them a brochure. One Sunday, I spoke to my mother out of frustration.

"Mom, what is the point of me doing this? No one is coming."

And she quickly responded,

"You sit there. They *will* come."

Her response sounded very much like the movie *Field of Dreams*, in which Kevin Costner was told, "You build it and they will come." Except, Mom had never seen that movie!

When I finally learned how to do a press release and created a website, www.HealingGardensatStoneHillFarm.com the numbers went from four or five each time we opened, to sometimes forty people, depending on the weather.

We decided to be open the second Sunday of each month, April through October, from 11 a.m. until 4 p.m. However, groups such as Bible studies, art groups, the Red Hats, gardening clubs, Girl Scouts completing flower badges,

CCD classes, cancer support groups, yoga groups, and others can call and make arrangements to come on other days. Sometimes families will arrange to come on separate days because of special needs, such as a visiting parent or relatives, or an illness in the family.

At first, the gardens were free to everyone and donations were gratefully accepted. When the economy declined, we decided we needed help to defray some of the cost of upkeep. The cost now is $5 per person, $10 per family, however, *cancer survivors are always free*. Donations are still gratefully accepted.

Not long after the gardens were open, I received a phone call from a woman I had never met. Her first words were, "Hi, my name is Nancy Chickerneo and we have to meet!" Nancy, a psychotherapist, like myself, was given a *Healing Gardens* brochure by one of her clients. The very next day, Nancy came over, and as we walked along the garden paths, she enthusiastically shared her vision of what she called, SPA Sisters. SPA was an acronym for <u>S</u>pirit, <u>P</u>lace (Nature) and <u>A</u>uthentic (self). SPA Sister Awakening Retreats, now called Awakening in Nature Retreats, would help others learn how to use Nature to sustain themselves in the midst of life's challenges.

I could see that she had put the flesh and bones on what I had learned about the power of Nature. She was in the process of training therapists to run the retreats, and I knew I wanted to be a part of her vision. I now hold *Awakening in Nature Retreats* at *Healing Gardens*. How grateful and blessed I am to witness the transforming power of Nature in a group of willing participants.

During the *Awakening in Nature Retreats*, after a short teaching on how to harvest metaphor from the things we are attracted to in Nature, the group is instructed to open their five senses and go into Nature with journals and crayons to reflect on what they find that is precious and valuable.

A mother whose junior high daughter was depressed, and considering suicide at that young age, wrote:

> *I am drawn to a small clearing beneath the trees where there is a statue of a mother and child. The sunlight brings a dappled blanket of warmth to me on this glorious day. As I observe the statue, I see that the child is clearly quite large and heavy for the mother to be carrying and yet she does. I feel tears arise as I think about carrying my own child, metaphorically, and I see the rock next to the statue which says "grace," completely summing up the only prayer that will truly define what a mother needs in this type of situation. The interplay of Nature and art created by man is profound. The statue is nestled between the limbs of a large tree, which has fallen, but continues to grow – its heavy limbs splayed in a feminine position.*

Another forty-year old woman who was sexually abused as a child shared these journal thoughts:

> *This journey that I am on is a healing journey. Today, I am drawn to the trees. I tend to feel alone on this journey, in this life, and when I sit in front of these trees, I see myself resting in the arms of others. One tree has fallen over into the arms of several other trees, which has allowed the fallen tree to still grow and sprout new life. I see myself in this fallen tree – parts of me have been broken, physically, spiritually, and emotionally. Through my darkest, weakest*

moment, when I could not stand on my own, God has put someone in my life to help hold me up. Along the way, like the tree, I have dropped seeds supporting and giving life to others.

As I walk, I see another traumatized tree obviously overcoming tragedy, however, the trauma has helped it to develop the majestic character that attracts me. I am a person who has been through trauma. I am a survivor. This tree has a story, just like I do. Someone could have easily cut this tree down a long time ago, because of the obvious imperfections. These defects did not keep the tree from growing strong and beautiful. The trauma I experienced doesn't define me, because I too, have grown strong and beautiful. This tree is worthy of planting beautiful gardens around it and being a gathering place to sit in its shade.

Besides offering a healing space in Nature for others and facilitating Awakening in Nature Retreats, the other important component of my healing journey is practicing Centering Prayer. I have now become a commissioned presenter and I am trained to give Centering Prayer workshops.

Many people ask how I am able to care for two acres of gardens. I tell them the energy comes from 'knowing' the healing power of Nature, and the deep desire to share this forgotten miracle with others through Healing Gardens. The gardens keep growing and evolving, as they are living, breathing entities that feed my creative spirit.

Being able to let go and accept what *is* and to focus on the present moment requires a practice of consistent quiet reflection. The benefits are a life lived with the eyes of wonder, joy, health, and opportunity.

Nature continues to be my partner in the 'dance of life,' constantly showing me new steps. Observing Nature has become a daily reminder of the way God sees me. The ethereal beauty of Nature touches my soul and connects me to the Divine Presence. It defies words. In a gentle way, Nature reminds me of the goodness and beauty in me along with the 'madness' and 'insanity' of my human nature. Thankfully, Eckhart Tolle reminds us "to recognize one's own insanity is, of course, the arising of sanity, the beginning of healing ..."

As I connect with the land, growing and changing on a personal level, I expand my heart to the healing and plight of Earth. All is sacred and holy. As James Hillman said, "We are then able to turn our human souls to the care of this soul world where we all have our home."

I remember the day Buzz and I sat in Dr. Death's office, two decades ago, the day I began to create my own journey of working daily on mind, body and spirit, defying his proclamation and leaving a legacy for my family, clients and hopefully, the world. It is not an easy journey, but is one I would take again. What's more, I know the journey toward balance and wholeness will continue for my lifetime and beyond. All I can do is take one step at a time each day knowing God will be with me whatever path I take.

Chapter 22 – "How To"

*"These people have learned not from books,
but in the fields, in the wood, on the river bank. Their teachers have been
the birds themselves, when they sang to them, the sun when it left a glow
of crimson behind it at setting, the very trees, and wild herbs."*
~Anton Chekhov

In this day and age everyone seems to love a 'How To' book of instructions – myself included. Therefore, this chapter is a 'How To – Use Nature to Nurture Your Soul" and suggestions concerning 'How to Deepen Your Spirituality.'

How to Use Nature to Nurture Your Soul

It is true, that simply stepping into Nature without thought or an agenda is healing, both emotionally and physiologically. Studies have documented that after five minutes in Nature especially where there are trees, blood pressure is lowered and muscle tension becomes more relaxed. It is equally true that stepping into Nature with guidelines and an intention yields a different, sometimes deeper, transformative experience.

I would like to share with you five simple guidelines I have learned over the past twenty years that have encouraged the nurturance of soul through Nature:

1. Before going outside set your intention with a short prayer, asking yourself what do I need right now? For example, you might need a quiet moment with no agenda, or you might be dealing with a specific issue, or your purpose is simply to connect with God, asking the question, 'What do you want to teach me today

about you, myself, life? Whatever you need, ask God to be with you and to help you.

2. Actively engage your senses. You have asked for God's guidance, use your senses, seeing, touching, tasting, hearing and smelling to become aware of how God might be speaking to you. John O'Donohue, a poet, philosopher and scholar calls the senses, "sacred thresholds to the soul."

3. Begin your time in Nature focused on *being*. This means walking without an agenda, being aware of your sensory input and maintaining presence with self. *Walk Slowly*. Let the Holy Spirit guide you. Perhaps you began with a certain intention and then became aware that your intention needed to change – follow your heart not your head. You will know it is your head leading when you hear, "You should ..."

4. Often the lesson God wishes to teach us becomes more evident when we use a simple creative activity while in Nature, such as journaling about our experience, drawing or taking a picture of what in Nature attracted us, collecting small mementos of our time spent in Nature, such as a leaf, flower, rock, twig or other natural items, or writing a simple poem, such as a haiku, (1st line, 5 syllables, 2nd line 7 syllables, 3rd line, 5 syllables or close enough!) For example:

> *Little brown acorn*
> *You have everything you need.*
> *You and I are enough.*

And, another example,

> *Please take me away*
> *Magical butterfly wings*
> *To the land of no thought.*

5. When you are finished spend a moment in gratitude. Remember, gratitude is a feeling. It becomes real when it is felt in the heart. Research shows that feeling gratitude in our heart for a minimum of twenty seconds changes the neurons in our brains, making us more open to gratitude and positive thinking as a daily practice. This gratitude practice deepens our spiritual connection.

How To Deepen Your Spirituality

> *"Just as a candle cannot burn without fire,*
> *men cannot live without a spiritual life."*
> ~Buddha

Over the years I have been asked this 'How To' question. First of all, we cannot demand grace from God, or answers to prayer by 'doing.' God's grace is always pure gift. However, we can place ourselves in a positive, receptive stance that offers the least resistance and opens a clearer path to receive God's grace. Therefore, our first step in deepening our relationship with God is a grateful recognition of this desire in our heart to grow closer to God and then, the prayer: "I am open, ready and yielded to your Presence; however, you wish to manifest your Grace and Healing." Now you have made your intention known to God and to the universe, so be ready to receive!

- Actively engage your senses while walking in Nature and follow the guidelines of 'How To Use Nature to Nurture Your Soul.'
- Develop a daily meditation practice. A rich spiritual life cannot be deepened without some silence and solitude in your life for reflection. (Centering Prayer is one method that is taught at Healing Gardens several times a year.)
- Join a Bible study or start a spiritual reading book club. Surround yourself with people who also wish to deepen their spiritual life. Be open to reading spiritual books recommended by others or from a review that you have read.
- Buy a beautiful journal, which 'speaks to you', or write in a special folder on your computer. Begin with the date and write, 'I am on a healing journey for which I am grateful.' Begin to write down feelings, concerns about life or maybe your relationship with God, experiences in Nature, or any questions you may have. If you are brave you can ask God, "What is it in me that needs to be healed? What are the areas of my life that need attention?" Write down the current lesson God is teaching you. A wonderful exercise is to write a 'Dear God' letter sharing your concerns, asking questions, even shaking your fist at God if needed. As in any relationship, God desires authenticity and can handle your anger. The second part is to have God respond to you. Fill in your name, 'Dear _____,' and write as if God were writing you a letter

- Pay more attention to your dreams. Especially dreams that are repeating, vivid or disturbing. I have found it helpful to keep a dream journal. Cultivate friendships where you can share and discuss each other's dreams. Go online and Google *dream symbols* to investigate possible meanings for the images in your dreams. Remember, it is only the dreamer who can verify the truth to a dream with an *aha* insight. Trust your intuition.
- Spend some time each day in gratitude for the blessings in your life, asking the questions: What am I most grateful today? What touched me today? What surprised me?
- Look for synchronistic events that happen in your life and know that they are not just coincidences; they are hugs and kisses from God.
- Investigate the Enneagram, which is a powerful, spiritual tool for transformation that will help you overcome your inner barriers and realize your unique gifts. Workshops are held at Healing Gardens. www.HealingGardensatStoneHillFarm.com
- Investigate ways you can be of service. We all have a God-given need to help others. Service is a natural outcome of a deep spiritual connection with God. The closer we are to God the more our motivations for serving are purified. Service takes us out of our ruminations about ourselves and into a deeper place of gratitude.
- Honor and respect your body as the home that houses your soul. We are told that our bodies are 'Temples of the Holy Spirit.' As a spiritual practice, take care of your 'home' by eating well and exercising. On the tenth year of my periodic visits to see my breast cancer

oncologist I received a direct order. A tiny petite woman always dressed in a Michigan Avenue suit and heels, Dr. Jamie looked up at me with a bright smile and announced, "You're fired! You no longer need to see me anymore." Holding my file in her hand, and looking intently into my eyes she continued, "There is one thing you *must* do if you want to stay healed, you *must* exercise."

I nodded, and then asked her, "Do you exercise?"
She answered, "Absolutely, every day."

Blessings on your journey!

Chapter 23 – Blessings

"...I know nothing else but miracles...To me every hour of the light and dark is a miracle, every cubic inch of space is a miracle, every square yard of the surface of the earth is spread with miracles, every foot of the interior swarms with miracles."
~*Walt Whitman*

I have heard comedians joke about people like me – people who say the cancer diagnosis has been a blessing and that they cannot say that they would wish that the cancer journey never happened. I will say that I wish I could have learned all that I did without having cancer! However, for myself, I don't think that would have been possible. So, here are the reasons/blessings from the power of spirituality that were deepened through a cancer diagnosis and why in hindsight, I can say I am grateful for the cancer experience:

- A profound awareness of how much I am loved by God and others.

- A strong desire to respect and treat my physical body with care.

- The powerful interconnectedness of body, mind and spirit.

- Learning to say *no* and making decisions that immerse me in soul satisfying activities, such as gardening, dancing, sharing my life's journey with others, helping others through my work as a psychotherapist to see what I see – the gift of who they are.

- Becoming more aware of my thinking process and knowing that my thoughts do not have the power to name who I am.

- An ability to recognize and stay in the present moment for longer periods of time.

- Slowing down, talking softer, using ordinary daily events like, waiting in line and red lights to center and ground myself, breathing deeply.

- More mindful of life without stressing out and more aware of what I cannot control.

- Becoming less and less attached to outcome. When life does not deliver the outcome I had in mind, I begin to wonder and look for the lessons and possible gifts the universe wishes to offer me.

- Reactivating and using all my senses to commune with Nature to develop a deeper understanding about life, God and my authentic self.

- More aware of beauty and a desire to create beauty through creative gardening and sharing the beauty with others.

- Most importantly, I have developed a tender awareness of my own preciousness in the face of my weaknesses and shortcomings.

Epilogue

"I would love to live as a river flows,
carried by the surprise of its own unfolding."
~John O'Donohue

At the time of this writing, Healing Gardens has been open for twelve years. People say the gardens have moved them and helped them heal. Some say they sense the peace and presence of God, that they have entered a 'Holy Oasis,' a 'Garden of Eden.' I know the prayers, grace and kindness of the people who have visited have left a piece of their love in the gardens.

Many of the lessons and blessings I shared in the previous chapters continue to deepen. I seem to have a pattern of recognizing God, setting my resolve to stay present, then a storm blows in and my focus shifts to fearful 'what if's.' I begin to sink, crying out for help and God rescues me until the next time.

Father Thomas Keating, one of the Trappist monks who authored the Centering Prayer method, reminds us all that the most important piece of this cycle is to ask for help and to take a risk, such as, stepping outside our comfort zone, i.e. quitting a job that is life draining, going back to school, leaving a painful marriage or deciding to re-commit to the relationship, taking ownership of the fallout from impulsive decisions, asking for forgiveness or something as simple as asking a question or giving input in a classroom or meeting. Father Keating writes,

The biggest danger in the spiritual journey is not to take any risk, we may think the spiritual journey is a magic carpet ride to bliss.

However, as I have discovered, the spiritual journey is really the crumbling and humiliation of the false self, the person we think we are. The Holy Spirit breaks through to all our secret places, which is usually a surprise, and most often not a gentle one!

For me, in bits and pieces, I slowly began to recognize my true self, the person God made me to be. God continues to break through my egoic thinking that touches on my need to be perfect, to succeed, and to be approved of and says,

> *No! Come as you are right now, with all your imperfections, and selfish desires. Come to me with your unfinished business and dreams, your insecurities and your fearful neurosis.*

What I do notice about myself now, is that I do not stay in the fear-based thinking very long. When I find myself there, I don't become upset with myself. I know God is taking me into a richer awareness and a deeper healing. It seems my greatest lesson in life has remained the same: learning to let go, to surrender to what is in each precious moment. In this process I am becoming a compassionate observer of myself, always trying to keep in balance my humanity with my shortcomings along with my gifts and preciousness. I find I can even rest in my broken parts and not be driven by them.

The cancers are in remission. In a *Healing Journeys* newsletter, Jan Adrian wrote about Kelly Ann Turner PhD, who wrote her thesis on *Spontaneous Remission of Cancer*. Dr. Turner discovered six 'treatments' that might bring about spontaneous remissions. I was delighted to discover I unknowingly embraced every one:

1. Deepening one's spirituality

2. Trusting in intuition regarding health decisions
3. Releasing negative and/or repressed emotions
4. Feeling love, joy, happiness
5. Changing one's diet
6. Taking herbal/vitamin supplements

Despite my five to seven-year prognosis, I will be seventy-three in October of 2019, twenty-four years after the non-Hodgkin's lymphoma diagnosis. I now have four beautiful granddaughters, Sienna, Eva, Makaylah, and Brianna. I have received grace beyond words.

That is not to say I don't have regrets. Going through the treatment left me with little energy for sharing with my children what was happening to me emotionally. At the time, I needed to process what was occurring and was often confused, afraid, depressed, in physical pain, and uncertain of what to share. I also carried with me messages from my childhood: *don't be a crybaby, suck it up, and take your medicine.* However, looking back, I wish Buzz and I had held consistent periodic family meetings, so everyone including our four children, Matt, Nick, Alyce, and Mindy could have voiced their fears and concerns, especially during the first treatment. Sometimes my fearful energy caused me to lash out at Buzz and our daughters. At the time, our sons, being older, were often absent with work and school.

As parents, we wanted to protect our children from the truth that this was a terminal diagnosis. Yet, they did know something was terribly wrong and they knew cancer could be fatal. For them, not being able to name what we were dealing with was probably scarier than discussing the truth. And so, I apologize to them now for that chaotic time in their lives, and for any way that I hurt them, knowingly or unknowingly. They were my motivation and inspiration to heal. I always carried them in my heart.

I would like to end with a final journal entry written six months ago, after a daylong workshop at Healing Gardens:

There is a sweet flow to my life – a sense of fulfillment in the ordinary ebb of living. I am doing what I love to do, helping others discover the same teachings from Nature that I learned – lessons about life and death, beauty, goodness, simplicity, sweetness, grace and especially, surrendering to what is and letting go. Today I witnessed lives change with aha moments in Nature, praying together, eating and sharing. Everyone has departed. The house is quiet, all cleaned up, dishes done. Bouquets of flowers from the gardens still fresh and vibrant smile at me as I pass by. I retire early, dressed in warm pajamas to our cozy bed with a good book – pure sweetness and joy. Amen.

Guide for Reflection

Reflection

Re-read the quote by Hannah Arendt. (p. 1) Do you have a story to tell that you would describe as *an intolerable event*?

Chapter 1

1. "God's 'overwhelming self' was all around me, and within me that night in bed." (p. 6) Have you ever experienced this sensation of feeling deeply loved and cared for by God?

2. "Through my studies and spiritual seeking, I knew there was a strong connection between the body, mind and spirit and I was determined to learn more." (p. 7) Do you believe in the interconnectedness of body, mind and spirit? Give examples of how they affect each other.

3. "This was our initiation into the world of Western medicine, where some doctors might know about treating disease, but know little about the human spirit." (p. 10) What has been your experience with Western trained doctors?

Chapter 2

1. "I was shocked into the awareness of this gross imbalance by the cancer diagnosis and yet, there was a part of me that wasn't too surprised." (p. 13) How balanced are you in body, mind and spirit? Which of these areas need more attention?

2. Reread the quote by James Finley (p. 15) How motivated are *you to look deeply into your nature*? Would you agree that it takes courage to identify our shadow side, the part we do not want to acknowledge?

3. Is it possible for you to notice without judgment your shortcomings or imperfections? For one day, keep track of your negative thoughts and how you respond to them.

Chapter 3

1. Describe a memory of being in Nature as a child, deeply engrossed in your imagination and play where time stood still for you. Journal about this experience.

Chapter 4

1. "As a first step toward healing I decided to journal about what I liked about my body now (a Bernie Siegel suggestion.)" (p. 21) List four things you like about your body.

2. "From my perspective as the third child in this large, Catholic family, with nine siblings, (six girls and three boys), our home was governed by three rules:" (p. 22)

Can you identify any positive or negative rules, traits or patterns from your family of origin?

3. "In the days that followed, I began to re-discover my senses, to *quiet* myself, to *look* at and *listen* to my world." (p. 34) Go out into

Nature and consciously activate each sense as you walk. Journal about what you experienced.

4. "Growing up, there was a lot of teaching about how much God loved us, however, there were also many rules about behavior and what would happen to you if these rules were broken – the possibility of an eternity of hell and damnation." (p. 41) What was your experience of God as a child? How would you describe your image of God *now*? I once read that *we become like the God we adore.* How true is that statement for you now?

5. "Next, Dr. Nancy took me through a guided imagery, helping me create a safe place in my mind, with the suggestion that I visit this place whenever I felt fearful and immobilized."(p. 49) Take a moment to visualize in your imagination your own safe place. Use all your senses to create this beautiful space. Journal about what you have created to the smallest detail.

6. "In my reading, I learned dreams, as gifts from our unconscious, use symbols from the conscious world to guide us towards our personal growth and healing." (p. 51)

Begin the practice of writing down your dreams and sharing them with a trusted spouse or friend.

7. "Thich Nhat Hahn, a Buddhist monk and prolific writer, teaches if you live in the past with rumination and regret and focus on the future with fear and catastrophizing, you miss the present moment and consequently, miss life." (p. 68)

Where do you spend the majority of your time? In the past? Future? Or in the *now*?

Chapter 5

1. *"What was I grateful for today?*
What was I not so grateful for?
When did I feel most alive? (p. 82)

How aware are you of your blessings? For one week ask yourself these questions every night before you go to sleep. Resolve to do more of what brings you consolation.

Chapter 6

1. Re-read the Wendell Berry quote about prayer. (p. 85) Have you ever prayed that way? Describe the experience.

2. "Being on the receiving end and knowing I need help is humbling, especially because I pride myself on self-sufficiency, a deeply entrenched Western world belief." (p. 88)

Have you ever been in a situation where you needed help but could not ask for it? Why not?

3. "I dreamed I was laughing at myself over something, I can't remember what, but I woke up laughing. What pure joy to laugh! The dream was telling me that a sense of humor is an important part of healing." (p. 100)

What part does humor have in your life? Can you laugh at yourself? Does your family call you the 'fun police' behind your back?

4. "This was not an easy exercise, but there is a *knowing* that tells me forgiveness is at the heart of healing." (p. 103)

Do you believe this quote is true for you? If so, list your reasons.

Chapter 7

1. "Like most who live in the Western Hemisphere, death was something I had no interest in exploring." (p. 111)

How do you feel about exploring death – your own death?

2. What does death mean to you?

3. What do you think happens when we die?

Chapter 8

1. "For me, synchronistic happenings are kisses or hugs from God, letting us know that life is full of mystery and surprise." (p. 125-6)

Give some examples of synchronistic happenings in your own life, as a sign of God's presence. This could be something from Nature, a song, a gift, a picture, a person, a book or phrase. If you are not aware of any, stay open to the possibility and look for them.

2. "Lent was approaching and I decided to ask God to open my eyes to any blindness in me. Sometimes one had better be careful what one asks for – because you just might get it." (p. 133)

Have you ever had a similar experience?

Chapter 9

1. "However, every morning I 'showed up' for my twenty minutes of Centering Prayer, which had sustained me during this cancer journey." (p. 138)

Do you have a meditation practice? If 'yes,' list the gifts that have come from your meditation practice. If 'no,' what roadblocks have kept you from including this important activity in your life?

2. "Lasting, life-changing transformation comes about through some sort of suffering or loss." (p. 141)

Do you believe this is true? Can you give some examples of suffering in your own life or in the life of others that caused a positive, life-changing transformation?

Chapter 10

1. Did you ever run away from a situation you could not face at that moment or needed a respite to think things through? Give an example.

2. Have you ever felt selfish for taking care of yourself? If you do not care for yourself, soon there will be nothing left to give.

3. "The whole experience of Europe became the birthing ground that opened me to the fact that I could never go back to my shallow, ignorant world before cancer, blind to the sacred, simple, symmetry in the ordinary rhythm of life." (p. 156)

Do you believe that our mundane, ordinary experiences contain the extraordinary? Give an example from your own life.

Chapter 11

1. "At my core, I am not a gut person, one who reacts to life with an immediate spontaneous, intuitive response." (p. 159)

We all have intuition – that inner *knowing*. How much do you value, trust and listen to your inner knowing?

2. How attuned are you in listening to the lessons God teaches in 'earth school' every day?

Chapter 12

1. "The speaker, Father David Engbarth said: *"We are an angry people who have lost our souls. We live in an addicted society. We are addicted to 'things.' All addictions keep us afraid and out of touch with ourselves. Our addictions keep us from God, as we feel worthless, a nobody. We are too busy to challenge this addictive system."* (p. 165)

Addictions can be hidden and subtle. Often they hide in things or activities that are out of balance – too much alcohol, food, sex, shopping, TV, Facebook, texting, gambling, worry, perfectionism, exercise, work, even reading. Can you identify an addiction in your own life?

2. "Finley said, "We need to *bow* and give ourselves up, surrender ourselves to God *just as we are*." (p. 166)

How difficult is it – to surrender to God just as you are? There is also a great freedom in surrendering. How is that possible?

Chapter 13

1. "Cancer and the debilitating toxic chemotherapy had forced me to slow down and learn the value of silence." (p. 171)

How much do you value silence? Why or why not? Is there room for 'stillness and solitude' in your life?

2. "It became apparent to me that we need two important qualities on our healing journey: openness and a sense of adventure." (p. 174)

What other qualities do you think are necessary for a healing journey?

3. "Pressing my cheek against the rough bark I could sense the essence of God in this tree – the strength, the energy and eternal groundedness. The tree, God and I were one." (p. 176)

Describe sacramental moments you have experienced in Nature.

Chapter 14

1. *"What is it about receiving potentially threatening news that turns spiritual resolve into jelly? (p.179)*

Have you ever had a similar experience? Describe.

2. "In that moment of reading the past journal entry I realized that all is well, that God understands, supports and deeply loves us in

our humanity. However, it is true – God protects us from nothing, yet sustains us in everything." (p.185)

How do you reconcile a prayerful request that results in a painful, unexpected answer?

Chapter 15

1. Re-read the Elaine Emeth quote. (p. 187.)

Have you ever found yourself in cave-like darkness? How did you find your way?

Chapter 16

1. Do you pay attention to your dreams?

2. Did you ever have a dream that helped you make a decision or point you in the right direction?

3. Make it a practice to write down your dreams, especially the vivid or repeating ones. Try re-writing the dream the way you want it to turn out – that points you in the direction of wholeness and balance.

Chapter 17

1. "The ongoing ticker tape flowing through my mind kept telling me that I am defective." (p. 203)

What messages does your ticker tape mind play over and over – such as, I'm not good enough, smart enough, pretty enough, deserving enough, fast enough, thin enough, rich enough, lovable enough and so on.

2. You can counter these messages with a huge STOP! Fill in with the message you want to hear in its place – the message any loved one would tell you.

Chapter 18

1. "We were taught to pay attention to our bodies and bring light and healing to the places that were tight and stressed." (p. 214)

How much attention do you pay to the well-being of your body?

2. Ask yourself what you are feeling right now and then notice how your body is responding to how you are feeling. For example, if you are feeling stressed, where do you feel this stress in your body? Is it across your chest? In your gut or forehead? Around your heart? You can then bring gentle breathing to that stressed part consciously letting go of the tension. When your body is relaxed your mind will follow suit.

Chapter 19

1. *"Can I really learn the earth lesson from the rose? To be? Rather than just do?"* (p. 215)

Would you put yourself in the category of a 'workaholic' – one who finds self-worth in accomplishments and not in who you are as a unique expression of God?

2. Today, can you spend thirty minutes *being* not *doing*?

3. Today, promise yourself you will check your breasts for any unusual lumps. Make this a monthly assignment whether you are a man or woman – males can get breast cancer too!

Chapter 20

1. "My attitude opened and yielded to absorbing and learning from Nature what I desired most – surrendering my own will to God's will." (p. 221)
What does the word 'surrender' mean to you?

2. "Frustrated, I often asked myself: *Must one always suffer to be transformed? Is that the only way?"* (p. 222)

Have you ever asked yourself the same question? What do you think?

3. Re-read the Mark Twain quote. (p. 226) Is there a desire stirring in your heart to change something in your life? What small step could you take toward making the change.

Chapter 21

"The ethereal beauty of Nature touches my soul and connects me to the Presence." (p. 231)

This *ethereal beauty* has a way of connecting the world of form and matter to the formless spiritual world. Nature naturally takes us out of our thinking minds into the present moment where we can actually hear the voice of God. Walk into Nature with this awareness.

Chapter 22

1. Discuss and put into action the guidelines in *How to Use Nature to Nurture Your Soul*. Better yet, attend an *Awakening In Nature Retreat* at Healing Gardens! (CE's are available.)

2. Reflect on the suggestions of *How To Deepen Your Spirituality*. Consider forming a small spirituality group based on the guidelines suggested. Also consider these topics for sharing: what lesson God is currently trying to teach you, frustrations in your prayer life, inspirational reads, questions about scripture, the difference between religion and spirituality, meditation practices, and so on. The possible subjects for group discussion are endless.

Epilogue

Have you also experienced blessings from suffering? Take one example of suffering and list the blessings in your journal.

1. "Father Thomas Keating, one of the Trappist monks who authored the Centering Prayer method, reminds us all that the most important piece of this cycle is to ask for help and to take a risk, such as, stepping outside our comfort zone, i.e. quitting a job that is life draining, going back to school, leaving a painful marriage or deciding to re-commit to the relationship, taking ownership of the fallout from impulsive decisions, asking for forgiveness or something as simple as asking a question or giving input in a classroom or meeting." (p. 241)

Are you willing to take a risk? If so, what would that be? Journal your intention and share with someone you trust.

2. *"There is a sweet flow to my life – a sense of fulfillment in the ordinary ebb of living."* (p. 244)

Is there a peaceful flow to your life? Re-read the quote by John O'Donohue. (p. 241) What changes could you make *to live as a river flows, carried by the surprise of its own unfolding*?

"No despair of ours can alter the reality of things,
nor stain the joy of the cosmic dance,
which is always there."
~Thomas Merton

Acknowledgments

Words cannot express my gratitude to Buzz for supporting all my decisions on my path to healing, especially my decision to stop working for three years while he handled the financial burden alone, and for helping me with the ongoing development of Healing Gardens. From the bottom of my heart, I thank him for dancing with me – literally and figuratively – through this cancer journey and our entire marriage. He has been my rock of logic, patiently listening to my fears, and then with a few words, grounding me with his realistic insights. For his generosity of time, listening to my concerns and his financial generosity, never shaming me for money managed or spent, and for his generous compliments and affirming ways, I am deeply grateful.

I wish to thank my siblings, Ann, Laurie, John, Ted, Felicity, Fran, Corinne (Bunnie) and Abby; also, Robin, Michele and Lynn, my sisters-in-law, and Jack, Terry, Jim, Mitch and Chaitan, my brothers-in-law. Their emotional, spiritual and financial help was life saving for me. It seemed as if the moment I voiced a need or concern, it was taken care of.

For my deceased Mother's prayers and spiritual understanding of what I needed, I am very grateful. My Mother, Corinne, was, and still is my greatest cheerleader.

My deceased mother-in-law, Mary, who I loved dearly, I give thanks for her loving support, sense of humor and her innate knowing of what needed attention and how to help.

A huge thank you to all my friends and friends of my family who helped with meals, flowers, gifts, working the garage sale, prayers and anything else we needed. There were many of you who I might not have thanked or wasn't aware of your generosity, please forgive me and know how grateful I am. Because of you, whenever I can, I pass on your kindness to others.

Thanks to Mary Conway who patiently transcribed all my recorded thoughts.

A special thank you to my friend, Joanne Spence, who read the first draft over twenty years ago. It was her initial positive response that gave me the courage to pursue my story.

To my women's spirituality group, Pam, Cathy, Peggy and Joanne, who prayed and walked with me every step of the way and also, encouraged me to write my story. To my dear friends, Dawn, Maureen, Sharon and Sue, I wonder sometimes how I could be so blessed to have you all as lifetime friends.

Love and gratitude will always go to Deb Beatty, who gave me a vision of what Healing Gardens could be and to Matt Klassen for his patience helping me with the website.

To Marianne Cirone and Pam Verner for your wonderful suggestions and asking the deeper questions, and to all my memoir group members who gave me the support and encouragement to finally complete this project.

Special appreciation needs to go to Kathy McPartland, a dear friend, who illustrated the book and created all but one sign for Healing Gardens, and to Bonnie Fruendt, my friend and consistent volunteer, for her weeding help and enthusiasm for the gardens.

To the "Crazy" sisters, Deb and Sue, for your encouragement and help with the Children's Garden.

Lastly, a giant thank-you to Susan Nunn for her editing skills, her positive support, suggestions, and her patience in seeing this project through to the end. www.csusannunn.com

Annotated Bibliography

When I was first diagnosed with cancer, I was desperate for immediate resources to give me some direction to begin the process of healing. This annotated bibliography lists all the books that were instrumental in my cancer journey to wellness.

After cancer treatment was over, I continued to read books that were influential and a critical piece to my staying healthy in body, mind and spirit. There were so many that were helpful, but it is impossible to list them all. Some of these I have included in the bibliography for your easy access. Wishing you well.

Anonymous. *The Cloud of Unknowing.* Johnson, Wm. Editor. New York: Doubleday, 1973.
> Written in the 4th century by an unknown author, this book speaks to your heart about the importance of contemplative prayer. A beautiful book, its timeless wisdom will parallel your healing journey. This book is a must for anyone desiring to enter the world of contemplative prayer.

Bolen, Jean Shinoda. M.D. *Close to the Bone.* New York: Scribner, 1996.
> For those of you who wish to find a deeper meaning to their illness.

Borysenko, Joan. *Minding the Body, Mending the Mind.* New York: Bantam Books, 1987.
> A highly readable and enjoyable book based on the author's work in the Mind/Body Clinic. She offers techniques and exercises to help you take control of your own physical and emotional well-being through relaxation and meditation. This is one of the best books

written stressing the importance of the body/mind connection and how we can take an active role in healing ourselves.

Bruteau, Beatrice, compiled by. *The Other Half of my Soul.* Wheaton, Il: Quest Books. 1996.

A compilation of essays, personal reflections, poems and stories giving tribute to Father Bede Griffiths in recognition of his contribution to interreligious dialogue. His Forest of Peace Ashram in India was Christian in faith, but Hindu in lifestyle. This book helps people open their hearts to a deeper understanding of Eastern spirituality and the gifts it offers to the world. We discover we have much in common such as our desire to transform ourselves into more compassionate human beings toward ourselves and the world.

Chickerneo, Nancy Barrett, Ph D. *Woman Spirit Awakening in Nature Growing Into The Fullness of Who You Are.* Woodstock, Vermont: Skylight Paths Publishing, 2008.

The author has put flesh and bones on what I have known to be true, that everything we desire to know about God, about life and ourselves we can learn through observing Nature. Combining creativity, humor, playfulness, and spiritual depth, she guides the reader through questions and exercises providing the structure to awaken, transform and nurture your spirit whether you are male or female!

D'Arcy, Paula. *Gift of the Red Bird.* New York: The Crossword Publishing Company, 1996.

A story about the healing journey of the author through a quagmire of grief and despair over a tragic accident. It is a riveting story of hope and spiritual renewal.

Dossey, Larry M.D. *Healing Words.* New York: Harper Collins Publishers, 1993.

A Western trained physician, Dr. Dossey researched every scientific study done on the power of prayer. Does prayer make a difference? A thought provoking, fascinating, uplifting, informative read.

Feinstein, David and Mayo, Peg Elliot. *Rituals for the Living and Dying.* New York: HarperCollins. 1990.

This is a wonderfully helpful book with exercises and rituals to help heal emotional wounds and work through fear of dying.

Fraham, Anne. *Cancer Battle Plan.* Colorado Springs, CO: Pinon Press, 1992

A simple informative book that helped me focus on what I could do each day to become a victor and not a victim.

Hifler, Joyce. *A Cherokee Feast of Days.* Tulsa, Ok: Council Oaks Books, 1992.

This is a lovely, inspiring, daily meditation book based on Native American spirituality.

Keating, Thomas. *Open heart, Open Mind.* Rockport: Ma: Element Inc., 1991.

Father Thomas Keating is a founder of the Centering Prayer movement, which has recovered the Christian contemplative heritage. This book would be the basic text for understanding contemplative prayer from its history to step-by-step guidance in the method of Centering Prayer. You will be encouraged to take the leap into experiencing Centering Prayer. If you pursue this practice, no matter what faith tradition, it can forever change your understanding of the Divine and how you respond to life.

Keating, Thomas. *Awakenings.* New York: Crossroad, 1997.

A deeply insightful book with short chapters on various scripture passages, this is perfect for morning or evening meditations.

Klein, Allen. *The Healing Power of Humor*. New York: G.P. Putnam's Sons, 1989.
This is a wonderful book to help us lighten up and take the first step toward finding the humorous side to our troubles.

Levine, Stephen. *Healing Into Life and Death*. New York, Doubleday Dell Publishing Group, Inc., 1987.
An important read for everyone, since at some point in our lives we will be helping the seriously ill or aged, and dealing with issues of pain, loss and grief. Everyone is encouraged to heal through a conscious development of 'merciful awareness.' Levine's meditations are beautifully scripted and powerful.

Linn, Dennis, Linn, Sheila Fabricant; Linn, Matthew, S.J. *Good Goats. Healing Our Image of God*. New York: Paulist Press, 1994.
This short, easy read, wonderful book can change forever your relationship and understanding of Father/God creator from one of fear/hell and brimstone to the unconditional love and mercy of God. It will challenge you to look deeply at your image of God, for "we become like the God we adore."

Linn, Dennis; Linn, Sheila Fabricant; Linn, Matthew, S.J. *Sleeping with Bread*. New York: Paulist Press, 1995.
The Linn's offer a simple, healing process for individuals and families to share each day. This process offers a way to get in touch with hurts and feelings, guide our decisions and help find the purpose in our lives – another easy read, short, inspirational book.

Linn, Dennis; Linn, Sheila Fabricant; Linn, Matthew, S.J. *Don't Forgive Too Soon*. New York: Paulist Press, 1997.

A beautiful book that gives a simple, healing process of how to stand up for your rights and be forgiving at the same time.

Linn, Mary Jane; Linn, Dennis; Linn, Matthew. *Healing the Dying*. New York/Mahwah: Paulist Press, 1979.

The authors say, "Because we have not worked through the fears of our own death, we leave so many to die alone – even if we do remain at their side. *Being with* is so different from *being there*." Through the seven final acts and words of Jesus the authors help us understand what is needed to die a whole healed person. This little book helps us to look at our own fears of dying and how to be with those who are dying.

Lindbergh, Anne Morrow. *Gift from the Sea*. New York: Pantheon, 1955.

A timeless read of the author's insights based on her experience of the need to come away and be still to develop an inner life "without which there is no true fulfillment." Whether at the sea shore or a quiet place at home, a meditation practice brings the gifts of balance, peace, integration and gentleness as we take the time to feed the spirit.

London, Peter. *Drawing Close to Nature*. Boston & London: Shambhala, 2003.

To help us draw closer to Nature the author suggests making art or drawing which is a creative experience that engages body, mind and spirit and produces a deeper meaning and remembrance of the Nature experience. Being able to draw is not a requirement to experience this profound level of communication with Nature!

Maloney, George A. S.J. Mary: *The Womb of God*, Denville, New Jersey: Dimension Books, 1976

A beautifully written book on the role of Mary in the Christian tradition. The author portrays her as an archetypal symbol of the feminine, stressing her openness to God and that we can all be wombs of God and give birth to Jesus in our lives.

Merton, Thomas. *When the Trees Say Nothing*. Notre Dame, IN: Sorin Books, 2003.

A compilation of Merton's writings on Nature that bring you into his way of seeing the world of Nature. His insights are beautiful, poignant and sacred. A lovely book to use as a daily meditation.

Merton, Thomas. *A Book of Hours*. Notre Dame, IN: Sorin Books, 2007.

A collection of Merton's poems, and prayers formatted into the ancient monastic tradition of praying the hours – dawn, day, dusk and dark for each day of the week. Placed in this format makes the readings rich, inspiring and soul changing. This book is to be read over and over meditating on the richness and beauty of his words that bear witness to the tender love of God, which is all around us.

Myss, Caroline, Ph D. *Anatomy of the Spirit*. New York: Three Rivers Press, 1996.

The author uses a model of the body's seven chakras or energy centers of spiritual and physical power incorporating the ancient wisdom of three spiritual traditions, the Hindu Chakras, the Christian Seven Sacraments and the Kabbalah's Tree of Life. Her fifteen years of research into energy medicine has led her to believe most illnesses correspond to a pattern of emotional and psychological stresses, beliefs and attitudes that have influenced corresponding areas of the body. This book will bring you to high levels of consciousness by providing you with the tools for spiritual maturity and physical wholeness – for me a life changing book.

Myss, Caroline, Ph D. *Why People Don't Heal and How They Can.* New York: Harmony Books, 1997.

As the title indicates, this book gives specific reasons why people don't heal and how they can in cultural and individual contexts. Myss teaches us how to disconnect from a culture of wounds and reconnect with an inner and outer spiritual energy and purpose.

Naparstek, Belleruth. *A Meditation to Help You With Chemotherapy.* Health Journeys, 1991.

The first part is a calming, reassuring, positive guided imagery CD about 20 minutes using your mind to help you heal. The second part consists of affirmations (ten minutes) which are powerful, especially if they are listened to everyday during chemotherapy.

Nemeth, Maria, Ph D. *The Energy if Money.* New York: Ballantine Publishing Group. 1997.

A powerful book written to help you come into financial wholeness. It will help you understand your relationship to money and heal distorted attitudes.

Nhat Hanh, Thich. *Living Buddha, Living Christ.* New York: Berkley Publishing Co. 1995.

A thought-provoking book paralleling the teachings of Buddha and Christ which are more alike than a Western Christian might think. The author is a beautiful writer, a poet, a Zen master, a monk, a truly holy man.

Nhat Hanh, Thich. *Teachings on Love.* Berkeley, Ca: Parallax Press, 1997.
This prolific writer gives us wonderful insights into loving from his experience and spiritual tradition. He presents love meditations and exercises to help us love ourselves and others. It will deepen your understanding of love and widen your capacity to love.

Nhat Hanh, Thich. *The Miracle of Mindfulness.* Boston: Beacon Press, 1975.
Eastern spirituality has given the West a great gift, teaching us the importance of living in the present moment. Practicing this daily has brought me tremendous peace, joy, and love of life. The author teaches us tools to be mindful and aware so we can attain this state of being.

O'Donohue, John. *Anam Cara.* Cliff Street Books, 1997.
The author, a poet, philosopher and scholar, takes you on a spiritual journey using the richness of the Celtic tradition to explore the themes of love, solitude, aging, death, the senses, as 'sacred thresholds to the soul,' friendship and work. Beautifully written, deeply insightful pearls of wisdom to help us on our healing journey.

Orloff, Judith, MD. *The Empath's Survival Guide.* Boulder Colorado, Sounds True, 2017.
A book that will help highly sensitive people understand their giftedness and how to cope in this, often times chaotic world. There is an Empath in all of us.

Peers, E. Allison, Ed. *Interior Castle Teresa of Avila.* New York: Image Books. Doubleday, 1961.
Teresa, a 14th century mystic, was asked by her confessor to write about her spiritual journey. Through

a vision, Teresa saw the soul as a castle in which there are many rooms, just as in heaven there are many mansions. She saw the soul as moving through many rooms before it reaches the inmost chamber, the place of communion with God. Even though this was written centuries ago one can identify with Teresa as she describes her spiritual journey.

Quillin, Patrick. *Beating Cancer with Nutrition.* New York: Random House, 1988.

This book (revised in 2001) gives ways one can support the body healing from cancer through nutrition. Continuing to eat healthy will help keep the cancer in remission.

Remen, Rachel Naomi M.D. *Kitchen Table Wisdom.* New York: Riverhead Books, 1996.

An inspiring collection of stories from Remen's life and counseling people with chronic illnesses that will lift your soul helping you to remember those times in your life when you paused and recognized the Sacred.

Remen, Rachel Naomi M.D. *My Grandfather's Blessings.* New York: Riverhead Books. 2000.

Another collection of healing stories from her relationship with her grandfather, dealing with her own chronic illness and counseling cancer patients that will touch your soul in a deep place. A consummate storyteller, Rachel opens her heart and pours out timeless wisdom with gentleness and humor. Both collections of stories I have read over and over especially when I need inspiration, refreshment and connection.

Riso, Don and Hudson, Russ. *The Wisdom of the Enneagram.* New York: Bantam Books, 1999.

The study of the Enneagram brings one to a deep level of spiritual awareness, no matter what faith tradition. The Enneagram will show you how to overcome inner barriers, recognize your strengths and gifts and deepen your understanding of humanity. This tool has changed my life.

Rohr, Richard. *Everything Belongs.* New York: Crossword Publishing Co., 1999.

Father Richard Rohr is a modern-day prophet who speaks a non-dualistic language. All are included in the infinite love of God; there are no exclusions. A prolific writer, I would recommend any of his books.

Roszak, Theodore; Gomes; Mary E.; Kanner, Allen D. Eds. *Ecopsychology.* San Francisco: Sierra Club Books. 1995.

A collection of essays from psychologists and ecologists exploring this new field of Ecopsychology that explores the reciprocal relationship between humans and Nature. How we treat ourselves and others has a direct relationship in how we treat the earth. These authors, along with James Hillman, see the world as having a collective soul and in that collective-soul-world each human soul has its home.

Russell, A. J. Ed. *God Calling.* Uhrichsville, Oh: Barbour and Co., 1989.

A lovely, daily devotional book written by 'Two Listeners' – two women from England who wish to remain anonymous.

Sanford, John, A. *Dreams: God's Forgotten Language.* New York: J.B. Lippincott Co. 1989.

For anyone interested in analyzing their dreams. Sanford takes a Jungian approach to looking at your dreams and shows through scripture how God speaks to us.

Sanford, John, A. *The Kingdom Within*. New York: J.B. Lippincott Co. 1970.

An inspirational study of the inner meaning of Jesus' sayings which will draw you deeper into conscious insight, that inner reality Jesus called 'the kingdom of God.' This book is wonderful particularly for those who feel dreams are an important key to understanding yourself.

Singer, Michael, A. *The Untethered Soul*. Oakland, CA, New Harbinger Publications, Inc., 2007.

A critical book that brings everyday conscious awareness by teaching the reader how to become an objective observer of habitual thoughts and emotions that keep us tethered in a negative, energetic prison.

Tolle, Eckhart. *The Power of Now*. Novato, California: New World Library, 1999.

This book goes deeper into understanding the wisdom and importance of staying in the present moment and *how* to be fully present.

Tolle, Eckhart. *A New Earth*. New York: A Plume Book, 2005.

An extraordinary book which explains the role of the ego, the part that keeps us a prisoner of our thoughts, emotions and beliefs that unconsciously we allow to name who we are. Tolle helps us attain a new level of consciousness.

Tyndale. ed. *The One Year Bible, New International Version*. Wheaton, IL: Tyndale House, 1986.

For those readers who wish to read the Bible cover to cover, this is an excellent translation. It is arranged in 365 daily readings which include Old Testament,

Psalms and New Testament which bring balance to the readings.

Williamson, Marianne. *Illuminata.* New York: Random House, 1994.
A beautifully written collection of poems, prayers and rites of passage.

RESOURCES

LivingWell Cancer Resource Center – Geneva, IL
www.livingwellcrc.org

Integrative Cancer Review – www.integrativecancerreview.org
The mission of the **Integrative Cancer Review** is to promote safe, effective and accessible mind-body and integrative therapies and resources for people affected by cancer.

Contemplative Outreach of Chicago –
www.centeringprayerchicago.org Our mission is to teach the method of **Centering Prayer** and to support those who's Spiritual Journey includes a practice of this prayer. The volunteers in our chapter are grounded in contemplative service – "God in us serving God in others."

Holicare LLC (formerly, Ton Shen Health)www.holicarellc.com
Holicare LLC practices Traditional Chinese Medicine (TCM) by means of Acupuncture, Tui Na, Cupping Therapy, as well as Chinese Herbal Formulas.

Awakening in Nature Retreats www.awakeninginnature.org
Nature based retreats and workshops.

Center for Action and Contemplation – Albuquerque, NM
www.cac.org Father Richard Rohr, founder; Mission: Amidst a time of planetary change and disruption, we envision a recovery of our deep connection to each other and our world, led by Christian and other spiritual movements that are freeing leaders and communities to overcome dehumanizing systems of oppression and cooperate in the transforming work of Love.

Made in the USA
Lexington, KY
02 July 2019